808.3/SKI ✓

CW00659756

FICTION
WRITING

WITHDRAWN

UCP Marjon

RECEIVED

2 3 JAN 2012

321638

UCP Marjon Library

321638

FICTION WRITING

THE ESSENTIAL GUIDE TO
WRITING A NOVEL

RICHARD SKINNER

ROBERT HALE · LONDON

© *Richard Skinner 2009*
First published in Great Britain 2009

ISBN 978-0-7090-8646-8

Robert Hale Limited
Clerkenwell House
Clerkenwell Green
London EC1R 0HT

www.halebooks.com

The right of Richard Skinner to be identified as
author of this work has been asserted by him
in accordance with the Copyright, Designs and
Patents Act 1988

A catalogue record for this book is available from the British Library

2 4 6 8 10 9 7 5 3 1

Every attempt has been made by the publishers to secure the
appropriate permissions for material reproduced in this book.
If there have been any oversights they will be happy to
rectify the situation and written submission should be
made to the publishers.

The extract from 'Riddles and Transparencies in Raymond
Roussel,' from *Raymond Roussel: Life, Death and Works* by Alain
Robbe-Grillet is reprinted by kind permission of John Calder.

Typeset by
Derek Doyle & Associates, Shaw Heath
Printed in the UK by the MPG Books Group,
Bodmin and Kings Lynn

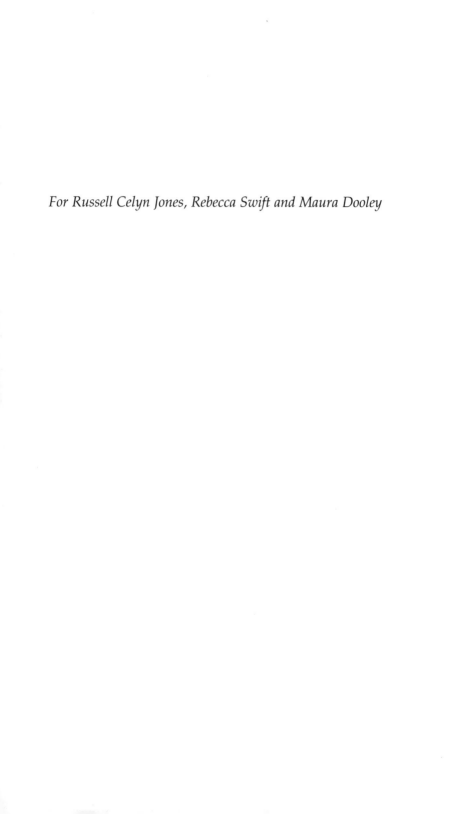

For Russell Celyn Jones, Rebecca Swift and Maura Dooley

Contents

Preface

'There are three rules for writing the novel. Unfortunately, no one knows what they are.' – W. Somerset Maugham

There is an old saying that writers are born, not made, but you are not 'born' a writer in the same way that you are born with blue eyes or black hair. For many writers, it is perhaps more accurate to describe writing as a 'predisposition', a way of making sense of the world, a talent stumbled upon rather than sought out. For others, this predisposition is actually a vocation, something they have known they will do all their lives, a need that comes from without as well as within. But, in either case, this predisposition does not mean that you won't have to work just as hard as you would if you were a fishmonger or a flautist. Writing is an unlikely, ephemeral occupation and your progress will be uneven and difficult to quantify, but you give yourself the best chance of succeeding if you dedicate yourself entirely to it. There are no easy options or short cuts in the art and craft of writing – the art is to be inspired and the 'craft' is hard graft.

It's also often been said that you can't teach a person how to write. While I agree that one can't instil talent where none exists, it's surely the case that creative writing tutors can draw out and shape what talent there is. By now, I think the argument has been won. Creative writing courses at both under- and postgraduate levels proliferate and flourish. These courses cannot (should not) tell people *what* to write about, but they can suggest *how*. Each text is made up of a subject, a structure and a style – the subject is up to you, but we can talk about structure and style. Some say that studying creative writing is the new way to study English literature, seeing texts from the inside out, as it were, rather than from the outside in. By learning the techniques of fiction, and beginning to write themselves, students see the internal workings of a book more clearly. They appreciate the art and craft of writing in a new, different way.

Apart from my own life as a novelist, I have, for many years, been a tutor of creative writing at Goldsmiths College, London, as well as a manuscript assessor and editorial advisor for a literary consultancy, all of which have informed my thinking and approach to this book. In my role as a tutor, I have been able to implement in my classes and tutorials many of the ideas contained in this book. From these classes and tutorials, I have learned many new things, which I in turn have put into practice in my own work. There is a symbiotic relationship between my life as a writer and my role as a tutor, one that hopefully benefits my tutees and certainly benefits me.

In my experience, the highly formulaic approach in most books on creative writing leads to a uniformity and homogeneity of style that, in my view, is neither desirable nor healthy. One of the most important lessons I have learned in my teaching is that one should promote difference and encourage originality at all times. I believe strongly in the ideas contained in this book because, in my experience, these ideas can help a person to write a good novel, but I have tried to refrain from offering it as a prescription. Nor have I made any false promises of success, as many books do. In the end, I believe that no one can teach another person how to write something as mysterious and magical as a novel. I believe the most, and best, a tutor can do is hold up a mirror to the students, make suggestions and point out the pitfalls along the way, which I hope is exactly what this book does.

The Structure of This Book

This book is both a 'guide' and an 'aid' to writing a novel. It is divided in two. The first part – the guide – will look at the basic aspects of prose and will offer practical suggestions for writers who are just getting started on a long piece of fiction. This part is based on my undergraduate teaching. The second part – the aid – has grown out of my tutorials with postgraduate students as well as my role as an editorial advisor, and will offer fresh approaches and solutions to familiar issues and problems facing more advanced writers.

In the first part of the book, I begin by looking at ways of generating ideas and how to begin the actual process of writing. Should you just start writing without any planning and see where it leads, for example, or should you plan the whole plot before putting pen to paper? It is vital that first-time writers quickly learn what kind of writer they are – organic or mechanical, night owl or morning lark. I then go on to discuss some fundamental aspects of fiction – what actually constitutes a narrative, for example – before continuing with discussion of various other issues, such as the differences between story and plot, the different kinds of story and genre, character, point of view, dialogue, 'voice' and setting. Insights from well-known writers and plenty of examples from published novels will enlarge understanding of all this material. I also draw on film and the experiences of filmmakers to illustrate how narrative works, since it is clear film and fiction share many tools and techniques and their narratives operate in very similar ways.

The second half of the book will be for more experienced writers who are well into a long piece of fiction. It will look at aspects of fiction that are much more subtle and therefore difficult to know how to deal with when problems arise: the role of the narrator, for example, and how much you should rely on the narrator to tell the story. Also, how exactly should time and the passage of time be handled in your narrative? Should you use ellipses liberally, or should you preserve the unity of time? This part of the book will operate more like a troubleshooting gallery – instead of offering definite answers to specific questions, I want to encourage readers to think differently about issues as they arise by means of lateral thinking, oblique strategies, aphorisms and quotations. I want to offer a range of ideas about the art of writing that stretches beyond the boundaries of fiction.

Introduction

'Art is nature speeded up and God slowed down.' – Chazal

The Art of the Novel

The novel in England was born in the early eighteenth century. It cast out the ghosts, angels, devils and miracles of the old God-fearing texts, such as the Bible and *The Pilgrim's Progress*, and brought in maps, clocks, calendars and human beings. Daniel Defoe's *Robinson Crusoe* (1720) is considered the first novel. Defoe was a dissenting Protestant, whose main belief was self-scrutiny. His activities as a spy give his prose an eyewitness immediacy that is the hallmark of his novels. With his scandalous book *Pamela* (1742), Samuel Richardson wrote the first epistolary novel in English. In protest against Richardson's supposed hypocritical moral stance, Henry Fielding wrote *Shamela*.

In the middle of the century, the very public disparities between these two novelists led to the bifurcation of the English novel into the 'internal' (character) and 'external' (plot): Richardson's *Clarissa* (1748), another elegant epistolary novel, still the longest published in English, versus Fielding's *Tom Jones* (1749), which used old forms of romance and rogue literature and was the first novel with a 'narrator' and a plot. Dr Johnson outlined the difference:

Fielding told you the time by looking at the surface of a clock, whereas Richardson told you how the clock worked. Richardson could have made a whole novel out of two pages from *Tom Jones*. Fielding gives rise to the 'adventure' novel, while Richardson sets the novel on its way as an exploration of interior life.

If Walter Scott gave the nineteenth century its dreams, then Charles Dickens gave it its nightmares. Dickens never stopped looking at the world as a child would, and the world he saw was horrific, hostile and hysterical. Gustave Flaubert was a slave to his art and style, looking for new ways to record the inner lives of his *petit gens* characters in provincial towns. Henry James, who was influenced by Flaubert, said of *Portrait of a Lady* (1882) that, 'the nightmare of Isabelle's reality is revealed in the darkness of her mind'. Flaubert's and James' work moved away from the social preoccupations of George Eliot and Thackeray and towards the idea of 'consciousness' and, in doing so, heralded the arrival of the twentieth century.

The continental drift away from Realism continues with Modernism. Novels are no longer written from the point of view of a disembodied, god-like entity; they now move inside the minds of human beings. Joseph Conrad is fêted for his narrative technique, which was influenced by James. After reading James' preface to one of his novels, Conrad says 'I sat for a long while with the volume in my hand, going over the preface in my mind and thinking – that is how it all began, that's how it was done'. Conrad's novels explore deep moral consciousness and are concerned with moral dilemmas, isolation and the psychology of inner urges. His stories are full of accidents, battles and death, told in a style characterized by complex time shifts, shifts in point of view, elaborate framing devices and densely written, syntactically complicated prose, 'floating uncertainly between Proust and Robert Louis Stevenson', as Frederic Jameson puts it.

James Joyce set microphones inside his characters' heads and used narrative as a huge microscope to 'atomize' time, analysing the present moment as no one else had done before. In *Ulysses* (1922), characters speak their mind, literally. In his work, Joyce allowed the unpresentable to become perceptible in his writing itself, in the 'signifier'. In narrative terms, Modernism tried to do everything *except* tell a story and looked down on popular culture because it did nothing *but* tell a story.

Postmodernism, however, says that, not only do we tell stories, stories tell us. The subjective realities of Modernist novels are scrutinized and become uncertain in Postmodern writing. Postmodernism doesn't seek to offer the truth as Modernism did before it, or that Realism did even more before that; it seeks to pinpoint and propose the ways and means in which the 'truth' is generated in a text. It asks, 'For whom is this book written?' A Postmodern world doesn't recognize hierarchies; it takes a hierarchy and turns it on its side. Rank is abolished, only spectrums exist. Postmodernism shows no respect for Modernism, only 'incredulity towards metanarratives' (Jean-François Lyotard).

World literature is the richest record of human consciousness. Lyric poetry is its most successful attempt at describing subjective experience, while the novel is its most successful attempt at describing the experiences of human beings moving through space and time. Human consciousness is self-consciousness: we not only have experiences, but we are conscious of ourselves having them, and the novel captures this self-consciousness.

PART I: GUIDE

1. Creating Ideas

'We do not choose our subjects. They choose us.' – Flaubert

So, you want to write a novel, that bright book of life, but where do you start? How do you fill that vast, blank page with perfectly weighted sentences, scintillating dialogue and characters that leap out at you? Before writers ever think of putting pen to paper, there is a fundamental question they must all ask themselves: just what is it that you want to write about – what is it you want to *say*? All books must begin with ideas and a desire to bring them into being, but how do you stumble upon that central idea, that spark or seed, what Henry James called a *donnée*?

Of course, there is no set answer to this question and there is no DIY manual that guarantees success. If any 'how to write a novel' book makes such a promise, it is not to be trusted. A novel is not a machine that you put together and complete according to a set of instructions, as you would build a Range Rover, or solve a Rubik's cube; it is a mystical, magical object whose creation is the result of processes that remain strange and mysterious to its author and that go largely unnoticed by the reader.

'Find out what you most want to say and then try very hard not to say it.' – Stendhal

A good place to start is to think about the kinds of stories you like. Which novels have moved you the most profoundly? Why do you think that is? See if you can identify any common themes between books you love. Any that you find are clearly those that touch your heart the deepest and so might be the most fruitful subjects for you to think about in your own writing. Andrew Motion, my tutor at the University of East Anglie, once commented that a short story of mine was about 'invisible others', a comment that hit me right between the eyes. In light of this comment, I thought a great deal about my reasons for wanting to write and why I was drawn to certain books. He was right, of course, and I have never forgotten this insight into my work.

Another way of posing the same question is to ask yourself what kind of book you would write if you knew for sure that it would *not* be published. If there were no pressure or expectation on you, what would you produce? This is a good approach to take because it emphasizes a crucial point for those about to embark on a novel, namely that if the central idea in a novel is one you care passionately and deeply about, one that is very close to your heart, you stand a much better chance of actually getting a whole first draft out. The first person you should be writing for is yourself.

'A work of art is good if it has sprung from necessity.' – Rainer Maria Rilke

A good case in point is that of the writer Paul Auster, who is perhaps still best known for his novel, *The New York Trilogy*. Most people think of it as his debut novel, but there is a book he wrote beforehand, entitled *The Invention of Solitude*, which few have heard about, let alone read. It is not really a novel, but more a piece of life writing, or memoir, a book about which Auster says: 'I don't think of it as an autobiography so much as a meditation about certain questions, using myself as a central character.' The book is intensely personal: the first half is subtitled 'Portrait of an Invisible Man' and is a study of his father, who almost certainly suffered from a form of autism called Asperger's Syndrome; the second half, subtitled 'The Book of Memory', is to do with Auster's feelings about becoming a father himself.

Auster wrote the first half as a response to the death of his father, so the two halves – death and birth – are mirror images, with Auster himself in the middle. The second half was, Auster says, particularly difficult to write: 'The more deeply I descended into the material, the more distanced I became from it.' He solved the problem, he says, by treating himself as though he were someone else and rewriting the piece in the third person. The book was, for Auster, a way of 'clearing his throat', the piece he felt compelled to write before he could go on to write anything else.

No one can tell you what to write about, or force a story upon you. Your stories must come from a deep place within you, but, because these ideas are such an integral part of you, it is still sometimes difficult to recognize them as they surface. In order to help you identify your subject matter, there are other means – 'coping strategies', as it were – that I have found useful for my own work.

Extensive versus Intensive Reading

'Talent borrows but genius steals.' – T.S. Eliot

Needless to say, all writers have to read, since reading and writing are two sides of the same coin, but it is not only *what* you read that's important, but *how* you read. When reading a novel for the first time, or rereading an old favourite, try to view it as an editor would, looking 'through' the text in order to pinpoint the underlying struc-tures and techniques at play. How does the writer bring his or her themes to life? What most appeals to you about the story? How is that dramatized in the narrative? Reading in this way can be a great source of inspiration and you shouldn't hesitate to use all this stimulation and motiva-tion to kickstart your own work. All writers 'steal' from others, consciously or not, and those who deny it are not being entirely honest.

Of course, it is advisable to read as widely as possible, but I have found that returning to the same book many times over can be just as instructive. The fact that completely different readers can be differently affected by a particular text shows the degree to which reading is a creative process. Any text has the potential for several different 'readings', and no one reading can ever exhaust a text's full potential because each reader will fill in the gaps in his or her own way, thereby excluding the various other possibilities. Novels (particularly Postmodern ones) are often so fragmentary that the reader's attention is almost exclusively occupied with the search for connections between the fragments. The point of reading is not to complete these connections, but to make us aware of our own capacity for providing such links. A second reading of a piece of literature produces a different reading from the first. It is not the case that the second reading is any 'truer' than the first – they are just different.

Your interpretation of a book is not burned onto your memory for ever once you have finished reading it. You might find yourself talking about a book that you only read once long ago and discover that your memory has retained only a few scraps of the text. You realize that, in the inter-vening years, you have reconstructed in your mind an entirely different book from the actual one. A book comes alive with each new reading. It is born again every time you pick it up. If you read a book many times over, it marks the changes in your life and, whatever happens, you continue to have a conversation with it.

Having read Paul Bowles' *The Sheltering Sky* a number of times, each occasion offers fresh insights into how and why the book is so well written. For example, at first I hadn't noticed how Port and Kit's journey starts at the coast, in a well-populated city, and goes directly inland, stopping at places that become fewer and further between and less well populated until, ultimately, they arrive nowhere, filled with nothingness. It is a subtle, sophisticated metaphor for their relationship. I also hadn't noticed that, although Port and Kit both have sexual encounters with native Arabs, it is how they respond to those encounters that matters, that defines the difference between their personalities. Port's is a one-night stand and the experience 'poisons' him and is his ultimate undoing. Kit, on the other hand, enters into a desperate, very physical affair with a Bedouin that rejuvenates her body entirely and sets her off on another journey altogether. Revisiting books in this way allows you to examine a narrative in 'X-ray' fashion, locating and identifying deep structure and embedded themes. Reading a small number of books repeatedly can be just as instructive as reading many books once only.

> 'In truly good writing no matter how many times you read it you do not know how it is done. That is because there is a mystery in all great writing . . . Each time you reread you see or learn something new.' – Ernest Hemingway

Mimesis

Take a book you particularly admire and copy out a page at random from it. Have a look at the flow of sentences. What do you notice about them? Write down any devices, effects or tricks the author uses. Write a passage of your own, using the same devices, effects or tricks. Sit back and read it through. Do you like it? Imitating good writing like this can be a good way into your own work, since counterfeiting is very close to invention.

Listening to a nocturne being played is beautiful, but imagine if you were forced to play it yourself. You would have to approach it in a completely different way. You're not so concerned about its beauty; you're thinking more about what you have to do with your hands in order to play it. This teaches you that the 'necessity' of writing comes before its beauty.

Thinking, Fasting, Waiting

This Buddhist mantra is useful for writers. You cannot 'decide' when to have an idea that will inspire a novel – the most you can do is prepare yourself in such a way that you increase the chances of this happening, and then hope for the best. Good luck is actually more to do with developing good habits for yourself, so do everything in your power to increase the odds of coming up with a good concept. When asked how long it had taken him to write 'Mr Tambourine Man', for example, Bob Dylan said it took about half an hour. Countering everyone's shock and surprise, he went on to say, however, that it had taken him ten years to get himself into the position of being able to write a song in thirty minutes. All you can do is be patient and as 'empty' as possible.

> 'Don't run after poetry, it penetrates unaided through the joins.' – Robert Bresson

In the meantime, keep a notebook and use it often. Write down anything that pops into your mind. If you treat this notebook as an extension of your thought processes, you will find yourself returning to it repeatedly. I have been keeping notebooks ever since I can remember, using them to store ideas that come suddenly to mind at the most unexpected moments, and that would evaporate into the ether just as quickly if they weren't written down: snippets of conversation, quotations, words whose meaning I don't know, diagrams, postcards, leaflets, lists, reviews, aphorisms, etc. During the early stages of thinking through and planning a novel, I find myself consulting these notebooks endlessly, picking out ideas and checking that I am on the right track. They are amongst my most treasured, irreplaceable possessions.

I also trawl through newspapers and magazines, tearing out and keeping anything of interest. After many years of storing such articles, I decided to impose some kind of order on my huge cache. I soon found that many of them were about related subjects and I started to file them according to subject matter, compiling a dozen or so folders: one was labelled 'Consciousness, Einstein, Bergson, Maths, Morality, Desire'; another was labelled 'Amnesia, Dementia, Depression, Bereavement, Memory, Mapping, Types of Love, Living Alone'; and a third was labelled 'Missing People, Recluses, Murder, Suicide, Zombies, Adversaries, Rose West, Myra Hindley'. I realized that each of these folders potentially had enough material in it for a novel.

Other people's life stories are a fabulous resource, too, so always have your antennae up. Some of the most interesting stories I've heard have been told to me in passing. The origins of my third novel lay in two stories I heard, one from a TV documentary and the other told at a dinner party by a stranger. These two stories – about a woman who has visions and a man who has blackouts – were both remarkable in themselves but, when put together, they proved irresistible.

'As humans, we test what we know to try to see what is possible, what our knowledge might lead us to. Writers organize those possibilities into stories.' – David Almond

'Tentative d'epuisement d'un lieu parisien'

One of my greatest pleasures, and sources of ideas, is going to a crowded place – a railway station or a café – and just taking in what's happening around me. People-watching is fascinating because it gives you huge amounts of visual stimuli to invent and build stories about the strangers around you. You could take this process a step further and write these sketches and short stories there and then, a process that would improve your powers of observation and description enormously. The French writer Georges Perec made a habit of doing this every day. He would go to a local café and sit, writing what he saw, making sure he wrote at least three sketches before leaving. He called this exercise a *'tentative d'epuisement d'un lieu parisien'*, which roughly translates as 'an attempt to "exhaust" a Parisian location'.

When in public spaces, listening is also key. What do you hear? How could you combine the sounds to make a story? What can you smell? In fiction, smell is by far the most overlooked of the senses. The visual aspect tends to dominate, but you should employ as many of the senses as possible in your writing. 'Qualia' is the scientific term for specific instances of our subjective experience of the world – the smell of coffee, for instance, or the sound of a waterfall. Looking at the scene in front of you via these sensory impressions will help you to see it more directly, as if for the first time. Familiarity is a great deadener, so take yourself to an unfamiliar place and ask yourself what it is about a tree that makes it a tree, or, to quote Viktor Shklovsky, what makes 'the stone *stony*'. These qualia are the nuts and bolts of fiction; they can bring a scene or a setting to life, so learn to look for them, especially where there seem to be none.

> 'The art really is in isolating yourself and letting as few things into your head as possible. To only admit those things into your head that come from a direction where no one else ever looks.' – W.G. Sebald

Writers have some kind of sixth sense about people, an interest in human nature that borders on the morbid. Or rather, I should say that their *books* display a sixth sense about the reasons people have for doing the things they do. Writers are trying to gain insight into people, to understand what motivates them, even when that motivation leads inexorably to self-destruction. But this investigation into behaviour doesn't mean that writers are better than anyone else at conducting matters of the heart. A mechanic might know the intricate workings of an engine and still be a terrible driver.

> 'Trust the tale, not the teller.' – D.H. Lawrence

Process versus Product

Writing is as much about the process as it is about the end product, and good writing is the result of endless practice. No one is going to write your novel for you, so you have to develop the discipline to get the writing done. When you're not in the mood, when you're feeling low, or when the weather is gorgeous, slaving away at a desk is not always an inviting prospect. Describing how she felt most mornings when faced with the task of writing, Susan Sontag said it was much like jumping into an icy lake – horrible at first, but fine once you got moving.

This process can seem interminably slow at times. A sentence here, a section there – it hardly seems worth it – but bear in mind that what actually appears on the page is just the tip of the iceberg. Those hours of thinking, doubting, clarifying, rejecting, rethinking are all contributing to your book. Sometimes you find that you have taken a wrong turn, or made a false start, or come to a dead end, and have to throw work away. This can be dispiriting, but there's nothing to be done except pick yourself up, dust yourself down, and move on. You learn just as much from a novel that doesn't work as from one that does. The lesson is just as valuable.

Your task as a writer is not to learn many techniques, but to learn the most simple techniques, and to learn them perfectly. With practice, the process of writing becomes more familiar. The writing itself remains difficult, no matter how experienced you are, but familiarity with the process means that the difficult gradually becomes easier, the easy becomes more habitual, and the habitual becomes beautiful. Be very sure – if you think a novel is beautiful, it is most certainly because a writer had slaved away for days, weeks, months to achieve that beauty.

Just Write

Another option is, of course, just to write, to start writing without giving any thought to it at all. For some writers, it is only in the act of writing that ideas are generated. The first hurdle to overcome is your self-consciousness. There's no getting round the fact that your writing will initially appear quite odd to you. Rather like seeing yourself walk for the first time, or hearing yourself talk, reading it back to yourself might feel like an out-of-body experience, as though it were written in somebody else's voice, not your own. There's no way round this – you have to start somewhere. Try this: think of an old friend and write for five minutes about the things you most like about them. Then think of what you did yesterday and write for another five minutes. Finally, write for another five minutes, trying to make a link between the two.

'Art needs white hands.' – Flaubert

The main thing at this point is to try to let any ideas come naturally – if you force them, they will elude you. The best ideas are those that are received rather than sought. Be patient, be prepared. Read as much as you can, letting it feed into your work. Stay focused – discipline is what will translate your talent into ability. Keep your nerve and the courage of your convictions and, when you have a hunch, go with it.

2. Planning

'Literature is the question minus the answer.' – Roland Barthes

When an idea has presented itself, your next task is to find a way of formulating it. This is often the most daunting and difficult part of writing and it is at this point that many give up. Asking a novice writer to plan and write a novel is asking them to go flat out from zero to hero. The gap between your ambition and your ability just seems too wide. But this may not be the case for long. You now have a great idea and the desire to bring it into being, which is a start, so how do you go about planning a novel?

Many writers come to the novel after having written short stories. It seems like a natural progression, but they are quite different beasts. Even the most complex short story only ever has about four main 'strands', or aspects, to it. Theme, character, action – all these are limited in number or amount. If a short story is like a string quartet, then planning a novel is like writing a symphony. Not only do you have two violins, a viola and a cello, you now have first and second violins to think about, more cellos, a couple of double basses, two harps, all the brass and woodwind instruments as well as percussion to think about. Walter Benjamin said that writing has three phases: the musical, when it is composed; the architectural, when it is built; and the textile when it is woven. You are at this compositional phase now.

But, not only do you have to face the task of planning an effective combination of all the elements of narrative, you also have to prepare yourself as a writer. To start a novel you have to be ready, able and willing, but to finish it you have to have staying power. John Gardner compared writing a novel to running a marathon rather than a sprint. This is a good analogy. A sprint is a concentrated burst of energy, but to run a marathon you need strategy, cunning, flexibility and timing, but most of all you need stamina.

Beginnings

Should you plan your story as a focus on the pursuit of excellence or on the fulfilment of targets? What about promoting sudden insight over sustained argument? In the course of a narrative, there has to be movement, light and shade, pace, but most of all there has to be sustainment and development of theme. These are the two key areas in any narrative because they are its essential requirements. Sustainment ensures that the story doesn't slump; development makes certain that it transforms itself. Taken together, they engender the narrative's prime interest for the reader and so they are the two most important issues for you to focus on.

Planning is a stage to help you to disclose the vision you have in mind via a text that is yet to come. If you don't plan, your first attempts at writing a novel will feel provisional; with a plan, on the other hand, you have a safety net as you embark on the high-wire act of writing a first draft. It is tempting to sit back a little if you have done a detailed plan, but it isn't your endpoint, just a means to an end.

'It is easy to plant clues and make a reasonable story out of

31

three seemingly unconnected facts because the author is
working backwards.' – John Buchan

If you are the kind of planner who benefits from preparing thoroughly for a project before embarking on it, you
might find it useful to go through your story visually. One
of the original, easiest and best methods of planning is to
write the numbers 1 to 30 on a piece of paper. On average,
a novel will have thirty chapters, so each number will
correspond to a chapter of your book. Against number 1,
note down your opening scene, and put your closing scene
against number 30. This concept of 'beginning' and 'end'
made solid should help you to envisage the intervening
stretch.

When you are going over what will take place in the middle
of your story, keep in mind the overarching structure of the
classic 'three-act' drama: the first act is the 'situation', the
second is the 'complication' and the third is the 'resolution'.
In Hollywood terminology, Act I is the 'set-up', Act II
is the 'conflict' and Act III is the 'pay-off'. Numbers I to 5
or 6 should set the story up and the denouement should
correspondingly be scenes 24 or 25 to 30.

In terms of providing answers at the end of your story to
the questions posed at its beginning, this structure should
read as a continual process of elimination. The first act
should show that the story could move in any number of
directions, the second act should narrow these possibilities
down and show that only some directions are probable,
while the final act should move towards one outcome
being inevitable.

'Entrances are wide, exits narrow.' – Anon.

With generic fiction, particularly when the storyline
ends definitely and unambiguously (crime novels for
instance), ordering scenes in this manner will help enor-

mously. If you are still having problems working out the chronology, however, take Buchan's advice literally – start at the end and plot your story backwards. Breaking down your novel into bits of time like this will help you to overcome the magnitude of the task ahead.

When American writer Chester Himes arrived in Paris in the 1950s, he was hired by the founder of the Série Noire crime imprint, Marcel Duhamel, to write a crime novel. Himes complained that he had no idea how to write a crime novel, so Duhamel gave him some advice, which, seemingly humorous and ad lib, is actually quite acute:

> Get an idea. Start with action, somebody does something – a man reaches out a hand and opens a door, light shines in his eyes, a body lies on the floor, he turns, looks up and down the hall. Always action in detail. Make pictures. Like motion pictures. Always the scenes are visible. No stream of consciousness at all. We don't give a damn who's thinking what – only what they're doing. Always doing something. From one scene to another. Don't worry about it making sense . . . That's for the end . . . Keep the suspense going. Don't let your people talk too much. Use the dialogue for narration, like Hammett. Have your people see the description. You stay out of it.

Himes followed Duhamel's advice and produced countless crime novels for the imprint, eventually winning France's Grand Prix de Littérature Policière in 1958.

'How can I tell what I think till I see what I say?' – E.M. Forster

Although some planning undoubtedly helps aspiring novelists, it is not the case that you must have your story planned and perfectly plotted before putting pen to paper. Famously, Nabokov didn't write a word until he had the whole book pinned out on index cards. Karen Blixen, however, said, 'I start with a tingle, a kind of feeling of the story I will write. Then come the characters, and they take over, they make the story. All this ends by being a plot.' Just as many writers only generate ideas through writing itself, so some writers (like Blixen) only find out what their story is once they have started writing.

With fiction that is less generic, more 'literary', it's perfectly viable to start *in media res* because you're never entirely sure how the story is going to unfold. In the planning of such fiction, you are confronted by a fair number of possibilities, and sometimes the best thing to do is just to go for one with a quick decision and then make that particular choice work for you. It takes you to interesting places with surprising results.

The danger of this 'free' approach, however, is that you have no reference points and can quickly lose your way. Such a high-risk strategy means that first-time novelists can often fall into the trap of indulgence, turning the narration into an over-egged pudding when it should be a soufflé. A meditative book, for example, may resort to melancholia, or a book about boredom can become boring. As a writer, your task is to convey the emotion, not experience it.

One way to avoid this is to try to keep all aspects of fiction in balance as you start writing. The four basic building blocks of fiction are action, description, interior thought and dialogue. Hemingway made great use of them all except interior thought – there is no interior thought at all in his early stories. Proust, on the other hand, employed a bit of action, a bit more dialogue, but a great deal of description and interior thought. In many ways, these contemporary writers are polar opposites and so provide good benchmarks within which to orientate your writing.

Endings

Endings of novels are, arguably, even more important than beginnings, because they bring a resolution to an enigma, relief to suspense or clarity to confusion, before transporting the reader from the text back out into the real world. Conventionally moral books, with their ends in their beginnings, are 'classic' texts, referring back on themselves and offering us a closed-circuit view of the world. Typically, they display a strong linearity of cause and effect and there is a high degree of narrative 'closure'.

They are books one can indeed judge by their covers, but the endings of some Modernist and Postmodern texts do not guarantee such a secure moral world quite so emphatically. For a start, the narration of events in the story might not be organized according to cause and effect, so that the narrative may be highly digressive or appear to take wrong turns. Also, narrative 'closure' may be problematic or ambiguous; questions set up early in the narrative might be left unanswered, for example, or matters left hanging. These kinds of text can have meaning but no point. They simply don't add up. They prefer aperture to closure; the comma, minor key and cliff hanger over perfect cadences, happy endings and full stops.

> 'A work of art should also be "an object difficult to pick up". The less it's understood, the slower it opens its petals, the later it will fade.' – Jean Cocteau

Critical Mass and Caveats

So you have done as much planning as possible – you have considered your opening and closing scenes and plotted events in between. Now that you have prepared as best you can, are you ready to start writing? Is this the decisive moment? While it is natural to want to get on with it and start straight away, I would wait a bit longer in order to let things stew, to allow time for the motivation and desire to bring your ideas into being to build up inside you until a critical mass is reached and you can no longer hold back. If you wait until this absolutely last possible moment before beginning to write, the energy released at this moment will be enough to carry you through several months, and will hopefully produce some good initial work.

One of the main tasks as you start writing is to usher the reader into the story as smoothly as possible. This might sound like an obvious task, but it is often overlooked. You can achieve this simply by placing us next to your main character. Where are they in relation to your background? Place us in alliance with your main character and let us see the story through their eyes. If you want to try to write a polyphonic, multi-perspective novel, that's fine, but the chances are that the reader will be dazed and confused from the outset. Try choosing one main character for now, and stick with them. It's hard enough finding a character's 'voice' and constructing a watertight plot as it is, so give yourself a break.

Another trap that many writers fall into while starting their first novel is what I call 'front ending'. The temptation for inexperienced writers is to pile all the 'story' into the first few chapters so that there is a car crash of events in the first fifty pages, or so, and nothing thereafter. Eager and impatient, they fail to see that these events have to be spread out evenly along the narrative, like pearls on a necklace, so that the story is sustained. In a narrative, time exists in order that everything doesn't happen at once and space exists so that it doesn't only happen in one place. Make full use of the spatio-temporal aspect of narrative in which your characters and story subsist.

'A writer is someone who can make a riddle out of an answer.' – Karl Kraus

Finally, don't think about the marketplace now. Instead, concentrate all your time and effort into planning well and getting your narrative off the ground. If you are keeping an eye on the market at this early stage, you will take one eye off the ball. Equally, try not to write *for* the marketplace. If you follow a plot blueprint that many others have used a thousand times before, not only will your story lack originality but it will come across as too 'on the nose'. Write the kind of book you would like to read, but also try to make it your own.

Print out and pin up a plan of how much writing you aim to do per day, week or month and work to your deadlines. Focus on the day-to-day, and soon you will find weeks have slipped by and you are well into the first draft. At the same time, ensure that your targets are realistic: if you aim too high, you will almost certainly fail and will feel disheartened; on the other hand, if you aim too low, you will feel that you are not fulfilling your potential. There is nothing like the feeling of a job well done, so work yourself hard but take care not to make appointments your abilities can't keep.

3. What Kind of Writer Are You?

'Writing a novel is like embarking on [a crossing of] the Atlantic in a canoe; after weeks of paddling you can't see the land that you left, but the other shore will not come into sight for months, or even years.' – Elizabeth Jane Howard

Apparently, everyone has a novel inside them, but very few manage to arrange themselves and their lives well enough to get it out. You, however, have decided on a plan of action and are now ready to set out on this journey. 'Composing' a novel involves a number of processes that remain largely unknowable to the writer, but the actual 'writing' of a novel involves hard graft more than anything else. You are at Benjamin's 'architectural' phase now; you have let the imaginative, creative part of your mind do its work; now you have to build your novel, bit by bit, step by step. As with any job, it is essential to find out the best working practices to smooth your progress as a writer. Are you a night owl or a morning lark, for instance? Virginia Woolf could only write in the mornings; Hemingway only wrote standing up. Settling as quickly as possible into a routine that suits your temperament will allow you to produce the most work of the best possible quality. Whilst working these things out for myself, I have found the following issues useful to consider.

'Eker' or 'Gusher'?

Do you like to 'binge write', to sit down in one long session and allow your work to issue forth, to 'gush' without impediment? With this approach, the quality of your work initially matters much less than the quantity. What is important is to get everything out, and do so in any order – the task of editing and rewriting can come much later. The important thing is to keep on going, not to stop until you have a first draft.

Alternatively, you may prefer to set aside a small amount of time every day and 'eke out' a limited number of words. This is a much more methodical and disciplined approach. Some writers are even known to stop dead on their target, even if they are midway through a scene and know exactly how to continue with it. When asked how much one should write every day, Hemingway replied, 'Always stop when you are going good and when you know what will happen next. If you do that every day when you are writing a novel you will never be stuck.' The advantage of this approach is that it isn't nearly so exhaustive; each sitting takes much less out of you so you have more energy for the following day.

Apropos this difference, there is an apocryphal story about Leonard Cohen and Bob Dylan. Cohen once found himself in Paris the same evening as Dylan was performing there, so they met for coffee after the concert. Cohen said that he had just finished writing a song called 'Hallelujah' and sang the last verse to Dylan, saying that it was 'a rather joyous song' (it isn't). He went on to explain that writing it had been difficult and had taken him a full year. This shocked Dylan, who pointed out that his average writing time for a song was no more than fifteen minutes. Cohen was speechless. Dylan must have liked 'Hallelujah', however, as it is one of the few songs written by someone else that he has performed live.

Flaubert used to spend weeks over a few sentences or a short passage, and famously spent days agonizing over *le mot juste*. The result is that he didn't write many novels (just three completed) and none sold well in his lifetime, but all of them have not only lasted, but are now hugely celebrated. Barbara Cartland, on the other hand, sold billions of books (she was named by *The Guinness Book of Records* in 1983 as the world's bestselling novelist), including society thrillers, racy 'bodice rippers', slushy romances and historical epics, most of which are hardly even remembered now, let alone read.

The point is that you must find your own *modus operandi* as a writer, the way of writing that will best precipitate your work.

'Some books are undeservedly forgotten; none are undeservedly remembered.' – W.H. Auden

Mechanical versus Organic Time

You also need to find out whether or not, as a writer, you are a 'clock watcher'. Do you perform best when writing between allotted times only – a few hours before going to work, for example, or at weekends? This method entails starting and stopping at an appointed time, regardless of how you're feeling. Sheer force of will puts you in front of your laptop, whether or not you're feeling up to it, hoping that you will warm up to the task and produce something worthwhile. This is a very 'mechanical' approach to writing time, an approach that disregards your body, but is one that many writers with busy lives have no choice but to adopt.

On the other hand, perhaps you will function better as a writer by listening to your body clock. Instead of appointing a particular timeslot within which to write, perhaps you should start whenever it feels right and continue until your body tells you to stop. This is a much more organic approach, much more attuned to your somatic impulses rather than your circadian rhythms. This difference is outlined in Coleridge's distinction between organic fusion of the parts achieved by Imagination and the merely mechanical combinations produced by Fancy.

We've so far looked at ways of aligning the writer in you with your personality in order to best facilitate your writing. Now I'd like to consider the kind of writing itself that you produce – style.

'Style is life! It is the very life blood of thought!' – Flaubert

Montage versus *Mise-en-scène*

In the 1950s, the French film theorist, André Bazin, set up this twofold distinction in film style. *Montage* is the French word for the editing process in film, the cutting together of shots – literally the 'mounting' of the shots. *Mise-en-scène*, on the other hand, literally means 'arranging things in the shot', and is the French equivalent of 'direction'. Bazin believed passionately that films should not be made according to some *a priori* plan but from bits of reality whose meaning could only be understood *a posteriori*.

Bazin's ideas gave rise to the *auteur* theory of cinema, a theory that attached greater significance to the director's personal vision than to any meaning created through cinematic techniques such as editing and visual effects. Bazin's theory pitted Realism against Expressionism; Flaherty, von Stroheim and Murnau against Eisenstein, Kuleshov and

41

Gance. During the 1940s, he said, Realism asserted itself through the films of Orson Wells and William Wyler and the use of 'deep focus', but also through Neo-realism, whose cause Bazin championed with special fervour. He particularly admired Rossellini. In the debate over Rossellini versus Eisenstein, the whole force of Bazin's 'Romantic' aesthetics comes out: natural versus artificial; organic versus mechanical; imagination versus fancy.

In terms of fiction, this dichotomy can be summarized as the difference between keeping sentences short and crisp, preferring to generate meaning in the accumulation of sentences, rather than by allowing them to expand in order to accommodate a number of images and ideas chosen to generate meaning within a single sentence. In the former, meaning exists *between* sentences, not *in* them. It says that, although a single sentence is grammatically complete, it is narratively incomplete. It is the *combination* of sentences that is a narrative statement. In the latter, however, there is an 'objective reality' inherent *within* the single sentence that does not exist outside it. The link between sentences is weak here; it is the *selection* of images that is important, not the combination.

'Sentences are factual, but paragraphs are emotional.' – Gertrude Stein

The Metaphoric and Metonymic Poles

The Russian formalist, Roman Jakobson, arrived at a similar dichotomy by looking at the concepts of metaphor and metonymy. He began by outlining the two basic principles and operations of language: selection and combination. In a sentence like 'Ships crossed the ocean', I select from a set of words and then combine them to produce a meaning. If I substitute 'ploughed' for 'crossed', I have created a metaphor based on a similarity between things that are otherwise different; if I substitute 'deep' for 'sea', I have used metonymy, which uses attributes or effects of a thing to signify that thing. Metaphor operates along an axis of language that Jakobson called the 'selection', whereas metonymy operates along the 'combination' axis. Jakobson developed this idea by going on to propose that metonymy is the general overriding principle in Realism (citing the moment in Tolstoy's *Anna Karenina* when our attention is focused on Anna's handbag at the scene of her suicide), whereas Romanticism is 'closely linked to metaphor'.

Again, Hemingway and Proust provide good illustrations of these differences. Hemingway's early writing consists of using short, crisp sentences that describe single, complete actions. In isolation, no one sentence carries much meaning other than the purely descriptive. With Proust, however, the sentences tend to be much longer, filled with clauses and sub-clauses marked off by semicolons, whose meaning grows so much that it almost tells a story within itself. We might say that Hemingway's style is founded on *montage*, while Proust's is rooted in *mise-en-scène*.

Hemingway himself once advised a writer to 'take out all the beautiful words and see if it still works'. The idea is that the less loaded the sentence, or 'shot', the more powerful the juxtaposition of two sentences, or the 'cut'. A blue beside a green is not the same blue as when it is placed beside a yellow, or a red. Not surprisingly, Sergei Eisenstein – the high priest of *montage* – posited a similar idea, which he termed the '*montage* of attractions', by which he meant that what precedes the cut should attract what follows it, and *vice versa*. The energy of this attraction could derive from a contrast, a comparison or a repetition. In this way, the 'cut' acts like the hinge of a metaphor.

'Poets are more concerned with arranging images than with creating them.' – Viktor Shklovsky

When all is said and done, however, you can no more impose a style on yourself than you can force a story. Your writing style will emerge in, and over, time. Some writers go to great lengths to suppress 'style' by purposely adopting wildly differing genres for each new book, preferring the genre, not the writer, to express whatever it is they want to say. Conversely, other writers use each new book as an opportunity to develop their own particular writing style, and a worldview that is deeply personal and intimate, almost as if all their books were actually one huge book.

My second tutor at UEA, Russell Celyn Jones, once told me that it was far preferable for writers to achieve success over a period of time rather than with their first novel. If their writing style and book sales slowly build up over a long period, the writer has time to assimilate this experience and adjust their expectations of the industry accordingly. Those writers who experience huge commercial success for their debut novels, however, find it difficult to cope with the size and speed of that success. The greatest danger is that they will not be able to live up to the pressure now put on them by the expectant publishing industry.

4. Aspects of Fiction

What is a Narrative?

This question may sound like a simple one, but it is actually quite difficult to define exactly what a narrative is. The term 'narrative' is a slippery one, refusing to be located or specified. The most common response is that it is synonymous with 'story'; another answer is that it is the same thing as a plot. While neither response is strictly true, neither is it entirely false. To understand how narratives operate, look at these four sentences:

> Peter fell ill.
> Peter died.
> Peter had no friends or relatives.
> Only one person came to Peter's funeral.

Even in this stripped-down version, we can see the story, but there is a central mystery at its heart: if Peter had no friends or relatives, then who was at his funeral? A secret admirer? A jilted lover? A previously unknown relative? The vicar? This is almost certainly the key to the story, but what happens if you change the order of the sentences? What if you put the last sentence first? Now, the whole story becomes a flashback, beginning with the funeral and ending with some kind of falling out between Peter and the other person. Now the story is filled with pathos as the rejected friend/lover/relative thinks back over their relationship with Peter. Likewise, if you put the third sentence first, the story changes again. Now, the suggestion is that Peter fell ill as a result of not having any friends or relatives. He pined for human connection but was refused. Then, at his funeral, someone appears, but it is too late. Now the story becomes a tragedy as we identify with Peter's fate. 'There but for the grace of God', we say, 'go I.' Despite this story manipulation, however, we actually have no indication of the period of time over which this story takes place. These four sentences could have taken three weeks to happen, or three years. Let's say, for the sake of argument, that the story occurs over a period of three months. As a version of Peter's story, how long does it take you to read these four sentences? A couple of seconds, perhaps five? So, it takes approximately five seconds to read about three months of a man's life. Implicit in this idea is that there are two time schemes at play: there is the 'time of the telling' – five seconds – and the 'time of the thing told' – three months. It is precisely this interplay between two time schemes that defines a narrative. Putting one time scheme inside the other is what distinguishes narrative from pure description (which creates space in time) and from pure image (which creates one space in another).

The film theorist Christian Metz has written extensively about what constitutes a narrative and explains the difference between narrative, description and image thus:

> [Compare] these three possibilities: A motionless and isolated shot of a stretch of desert is an image; several partial and successive shots of this desert waste make up a description; several successive shots of a caravan moving across the desert constitute a narrative.

If narratives are defined by their temporal aspect, it follows that only the 'temporal' arts possess narratives.

46

Prose, music, film, theatre, poetry, dance – all these art forms require a 'time of the telling' in order for their stories to unfold; the 'plastic' arts – painting, sculpture, pottery, dressmaking and architecture, for example – do not. You are not required to stand in front of a painting for a specific length of time in order to understand or appreciate it. You may look at a painting for one minute or one hour, it is entirely your decision. A painting does not possess a 'time of the telling' and so, when art critics talk about the 'narrative' within a painting, the term is a misnomer since paintings are images and are therefore creating spaces within spaces, not one time scheme within another.

The same issue arises with texts that contain huge tracts of description. An example of a descriptive non-fiction text in its purest form would be an instruction manual or a guidebook, which have absolutely no need for a 'time of the telling'. In novels, description works in fundamental opposition to narrative flow. In fiction, when you read a description of a person or place, the 'time of the thing told' pauses and another aspect of writing takes over. Writing description is spending time describing space.

On occasion, this style of writing is taken to an extreme, as in Alain Robbe-Grillet's *Jealousy*. The setting is a banana plantation in some unnamed tropical country. The story is seen through the eyes of a narrator who is never named (though he is often addressed), never speaks and never acts. The first-person pronoun is never used and the narrator's only role is to observe the other two characters – his wife and their neighbour (with whom the narrator suspects his wife is having an affair) – in and around the couple's plantation house. The text is full of highly descriptive attention to detail: examining posture and gesture, sometimes in extreme close-up; seeing an action repeated from one or several different points of view; describing the relations between objects in a landscape; noting the progress of shadows thrown by the sun; exploring texture (bark, cloth,

47

paint) and sound. All action is broken down, re-examined, contradicted, and the story is kept at arm's length, pinned down, like a butterfly in a cabinet, never allowed to be more than a *tableau vivant*.

Depicting things in this flat way empties them of human significance; the writing becomes purely self-reflexive. For his investigations into the pure surface of things, Robbe-Grillet found inspiration in the writings of Raymond Roussel, whose work early in the twentieth century greatly influenced a number of French *nouveau roman* writers who wished to challenge received notions of narrative. Of Roussel's work, Robbe-Grillet wrote:

> As there is never anything beyond the thing described . . . the reader's eye is forced to fall on the surface of things . . . Such total transparency, which leaves neither shadow nor reflection behind it, in fact turns into a *trompe-l'oeil* painting. The greater the accumulation of minutiae, of details of forms and dimensions, the more the object loses its depth. So this is an opacity without mystery, just as there is nothing behind the surface of a backcloth, no inside, no secret; no ulterior motive . . .
>
> Empty enigmas, time standing still, signs that refuse to be significant, gigantic enlargements of minute details, tales that turn in on themselves, we are in a flat and discontinuous universe where everything refers only to itself. A universe of fixity, of repetition, of absolute clarity, which enchants and discourages the explorer . . .

Chatman's diagram

Now that we've defined what a narrative is, let's look inside a narrative, as it were, to see what's going on. The best-known, and still useful, attempt to identify accurately the complex set of interactions between a writer and a reader through a work of fiction is the following diagram suggested by Seymour Chatman:

NARRATIVE TEXT

Chatman proposed this diagram primarily because he wanted to illustrate the differences between 'author' and 'narrator', terms that are often mistakenly thought to be one and the same. It is convention to ignore the real author (D.H. Lawrence's 'Trust the tale, not the teller'), but it is impossible to disregard the narrator. It doesn't matter if the narrator of a story is a character who plays a significant role within it (Marlow in Conrad's *Heart of Darkness*, for example), or a character who takes no real part in the action (Nick Carraway in Fitzgerald's *The Great Gatsby*, for instance), or whether he or she is not actually a character in the story at all (as in Hemingway's early stories). The fact of the narrator's presence is irrefutable.

The 'implied author'
'A text's unity lies not in its origin but in its destination.' –
Roland Barthes

The term that has created the most confusion in this diagram is the 'implied author', a term coined by literary theorist Wayne Booth. As we've seen, there is a difference between author and narrator, but what defines that difference? For the handful of writers who are very much in the public eye, readers will obviously have some idea of what kind of people they are. When a writer becomes famous (as opposed to successful), celebrity can outweigh craft and it is often hard for their readers to continue to believe in that writer's creations. When reading their books, we are too aware of the personality behind them, so much so that the presence of the real author can distract and deter us from the reading process. When fame hits hard like this, writers often complain that their anonymity has been taken from them.

The majority of writers have no such problem, however. Even if a reader knows a few biographical details about them before reading their books, they usually do not, and will never, know very much about them. But this doesn't stop readers from forming an impression of the author while reading. They might ask themselves 'What kind of person would write this book?' or 'Why?' The gap between real author and narrator is inhabited by this 'implied author', which is the reader's inkling of what the author must be like based on these impressions and ideas.

Although the author ultimately has no control over such impressions, they can still play with this notion. An 'implied author' is a version of the author, their second self, mask or persona, the person responsible for the design and values of a text. This alter ego could be a twin, a doppelgänger, a dummy, a forger, a decoy or a stand-in, depending on how an author wishes to cast themselves in the minds of their readers. How often do we see a writer we have long admired being interviewed only to feel disappointed? 'I thought she would be funnier,' we think, or 'How fragile and frail he seems.' Such play can only really take place if the writer preserves some degree of anonymity, though – it gets proportionally harder the more fixed you become in the public eye.

But none of this really matters, or at least it shouldn't. As the Roland Barthes quotation implies, a text is significant only because of where it takes the reader, not whence it came. The author is dead! Long live the author!

The 'narratee'

Just as there is always someone who narrates, so there must equally be a person to whom the narrator addresses the story (the 'narratee'). Usually, the narratee is not identified by name; they are just assumed to be there, present in the narrative so that the story can be heard or read. The very fact that someone listens to, or reads, a story means that it exists – stories would not survive without their readers and listeners.

The most obvious role of the narratee in the text is as a 'relay' between narrator and reader. Whenever there is an ambiguity within the story, or its narration, the narrator can directly address the narratee with a clarification, knowing that the reader will pick up this information too. Such explicit 'asides' were used a great deal when the novel was in its infancy – by Fielding in *Tom Jones*, for example, and by Laurence Sterne in *Tristram Shandy* (1759). The narratee's role in *Tristram Shandy*, however, is taken a stage further by having the narratee identified as a particular individual, a woman Sterne calls 'Madam'. While she has no voice of her own in the narrative, we can infer her contributions to the one-sided conversation from the narrator's lines: 'How could you, Madam, be so inattentive in reading the last chapter? I told you in it, *That my mother was not a papist.*'

Since Fielding and Sterne, novelists have given the narratee many other roles. Conrad's *Heart of Darkness* (1902), for example, is constructed as a 'framed' narrative, whereby one narrative sits inside another. In the book, the first, unnamed narrator recounts how he once found himself with a group of people waiting on a boat for the tide to turn on the Thames. To pass the time, one of the group, a man named Marlow, proposes to tell them a story, the details of which the anonymous narrator relays to us. Thus Marlow is not the original narrator, and the story he tells is told second-hand. In his own narrative, Marlow is a 'dramatized' narrator, by which I mean he has experienced the events as a character, not merely as an observer. The moment he starts listening to Marlow's story, however, the original narrator becomes narratee and plays no other role for the rest of the story.

Sometimes, the narratee of a story can, at the same time, be its narrator. In Jean-Paul Sartre's *Nausea* (1938), for example, Roquentin doesn't intend his narrative to be heard by anyone other than himself because the narrative is comprised solely of his diary, of which he is the only reader. On other occasions, texts may appear to have no narratee at all. The detached prose style in Albert Camus' *The Outsider* (1942), for example, ensures that Mersault remains distant from events in the book, and from himself. The deep solitude that lies at the heart of his character means that Mersault does not know how to interact socially or engage in a real dialogue with anyone, including a narratee. Although we are reading, the narratee in Camus' book is not sensed, either by us or by Mersault himself.

Postmodernism brings back into play a tendency for direct address between narrator and narratee. In Italo Calvino's *If on a Winter's Night a Traveller* (1979), for instance, the narrator addresses the narratee (and, by proxy, the reader) directly throughout the book, beginning 'You are about to begin reading Italo Calvino's new novel, *If on a Winter's Night a Traveller*. Relax. Concentrate. Dispel every other thought. Let the world around you fade.' For Calvino, this toying with the role a narratee plays in a text highlights the explicitly artificial nature of narrative.

By and large, however, such 'tricksy', 'dramatized' or 'blank' roles assigned to the narratee are unusual. In most novels, it is much more common for writers to assume their stories are naturally being addressed to someone within the textual world, as well as the reader. Unless you deliberately want to start experimenting with form, it is probably wisest at this stage to stick with convention.

Story versus Plot

The difference between story and plot is one of the issues that causes the most consternation and vexation for those writers just starting out. Again, the best way to illustrate the difference is by example:

> The dog came out of the forest. The man left the door open. The dog came out of the forest. The man had left the door open.

What is the difference between these two examples? In the first quotation, is there a link between the two events? Did the man leave the door open *because* the dog came out of the forest? Maybe. What about the second quotation – does the tense change make a difference? The answer is yes, it clearly does. The change of tense in the second sentence suggests a greater connection between the dog coming out of the forest and the man leaving the door open. Making that grammatical change from the simple past (left) to the past perfect (had left) tells us that the man's door was left open *before* the dog came out of the forest; indeed, the assumption is that the man left the door open precisely because he *knew* the dog would come out of the forest and was waiting for it to do so. The connection in the first quotation is more tenuous. It may be the case that the man saw the dog leave the forest and opened his door as a result, or it could be that the two events are not connected at all – the link is not strong.

In this example, the first quotation is a story, the second a plot, and this sense of causality in the second quotation is what defines a plot. In a plot, things happen *because of* what has come before, not *in spite of* it; in a story, however, things 'just happen'. Think of the way children tell stories – they have little sense of plot: 'This happened and then this happened and then this happened . . .' Children have yet to learn how to order events for the benefit of the listener; the chronology of events is preserved but their stories show no sense of causality, and so they remain merely episodic.

Another, much more famous, example to show the difference between story and plot was posited by E.M. Forster in 1927:

> The King died and then the Queen died.
> The King died, and then the Queen died of grief.

In the first sentence, we understand the order of events but not necessarily the link between them. Did the Queen die *because* the King did? Perhaps not. In the second sentence, however, the link is made strongly and clearly – yes, the Queen died *because* the King did. The second sentence now possesses cause and effect and we now know the difference between what happens merely consecutively and what happens as a direct consequence of what came before. A story is made out of events, but a plot makes events into a story. Plot leads you through a narrative, whereas you merely follow the story.

In our definition of what constitutes a narrative, the 'time of the telling' would be synonymous with plot and the 'time of the thing told' with story. The Russian Formalists called story *fabula* and the plot *sjuzhet*. French *narratologistes* label story *histoire* and plot *récit.* Anglo-American Post-structuralists, however, somewhat confusingly refer to plot as 'discourse'. But, by whatever name they are called, the differences between the two are the same. Whatever the story may be, its plot is its engine, its impetus. The causality of a plot ensures forward movement, not circular motion, progression, not repetition. Plot is the driving force within a narrative, moving the reader and the story forward towards the end, while simultaneously delaying that end.

Character-led and plot-led fiction have traditionally been used by publishers in particular, and the industry in general, to differentiate between 'literary' and 'commercial' fiction respectively. Somehow, fiction that is plot-driven has, over the years, become synonymous with poorer quality, cheapness, contempt even, but this is a huge error of judgement. Malign it if you will, but ignore it at your peril, for plot is the 'thrust' of a narrative, and its genetic code – without it, a narrative seems lifeless, without energy, inert. A narrative that is weakly plotted feels as though it will never get started, and then you think it is never going to end.

'When I am thickening my plots, I like to think "What if . . . What if . . ." ' – Patricia Highsmith

A narrative that is driven by a plot whose chain of events has not been sufficiently linked can end up feeling broken-backed or fractured, but it is also possible to end up with a plot that is too 'busy'. Plots that are 'cluttered' in this way are overdetermined in the sense that each point possesses a multiplicity of causes and suggests a plurality of meanings. Fractured plots can leave the reader feeling bored, but plots that are cluttered in this way can leave them feeling bewildered, which is just as damaging. So where to draw the fine line between the two?

When thinking about plotting, the first thing to do is to get your story straight. The 'story' in any narrative has to have a few fundamental questions addressed and answered during its course in order to ensure basic comprehension. Put simply, these are: 'who', 'what', 'when' and 'where' (referring to characters, action, period and setting respectively). For now, leave the 'why' (motivation) out of it. Barthes referred to the who, what, when and where of a narrative as its 'denotation' and the 'why' as its 'connotation'. Deciding why the characters do what they do is the reader's job, but the denotation is a writer's first business – what is going to happen? To whom? When? Where? These are the basic components of your story and they need to be sorted out before anything else.

Once you have your story, you need to decide in what order you are going to place those events. Putting them in different orders will create different effects. Even in our very simple example of three months in the life of Peter, placing events in three different orders created three different effects. Are you going to tell your story logically or chronologically? Plot is the logic and dynamic of narrative, and this logical dynamic isn't duty-bound to preserve chronology. The weaker the causal connection in plot, the stronger the purely chronological connection.

Crime novels are a good example to look at when talking about plot, as they are perhaps the most purely plot-driven kind of fiction. Other kinds answer their denotative questions almost immediately, but crime fiction places the who, what, when and where under scrutiny from the very outset. The point of a crime novel is to delay these answers until the end of the narrative. Some pose a series of questions that look forward into the future for their answers; others work by asking questions that delve into the past. Anticipatory narratives operate via surprise and suspense and are usually labelled 'thrillers'; retrospective narratives work via the set-up and solution to a mystery and are what we call 'whodunits'. The logic of the whodunit necessitates that a body turn up at the beginning of its narrative (although, thanks to our meticulous plotting, the murder may not have occurred at the beginning the story), and proceeds by ranging back and forth over time from this initial effect to find its cause. Thrillers, however, usually work by making us identify closely with the hero at the beginning of the story and then keeping us in close proximity as he or she works from cause to effect and eventually arrives at the truth, preserving chronology along the way.

As a writer, Hemingway preferred to find 'grace under pressure' among soldiers and hunters rather than in the world of small-time crooks and cops, but his short story 'The Killers' is one of the best crime short stories there is. Two men in black overcoats and derby hats enter a diner in a small town. The owner asks them for their order, but the two men don't know what they want. It eventually transpires that they are there to assassinate one of the regulars at the diner. What follows is a masterclass in veiled threats and subtle shifts in power as the two men assert their authority and control over the owner, the cook, and a customer called Nick Adams – all done almost entirely through menacing, Pinteresque dialogue. The situation is a kind of foreshortened version of Michael Haneke's *Funny Games*, with violence threatening to erupt at any time and the story seething with tension. And all this in just six pages.

For highly plot-driven genre fiction like this, the plot is advanced through words and actions rather than by any reflection on the character's part (this is Hemingway's 'signature' style in his early stories). If something happens once, it's an accident, but if it happens twice, it's a pattern. Such repetition of events can mark changes, both in the story and to characters. Plotting is all about the patterning of events in order to create effects. Switching events around can cause little bombs of surprise and suspense to detonate in different places in your narrative. Such moments of surprise and suspense are the points around which the plot turns. Plot shows us the cogs and pulleys of narrative, the *j'accuses* and, eventually, the *mea culpas*.

Once you have done your plotting, you need to think about each scene individually. A well-plotted narrative is constructed by putting together a series of linked scenes, but each scene in this series should be built up as dramatically as possible, by which I mean that the narrator ought, as much as possible, to let us see for ourselves what the characters say and do without interpreting for our benefit whatever the narrator thinks those words and actions might mean. The most effective way for an author to engage and involve the reader to a very high degree is to let the story (the words and actions of the characters) speak for itself. We need to see the story, not have it *told* to us – 'Show, don't tell.'

Furthermore, not only should each scene in your narrative be as beautifully realized and achieved as possible in itself, but it should also serve to sustain and develop the story as a whole. As we start reading each new scene, we should find it both surprising and inevitable – surprising because it should offer us an unusual angle on, or an additional twist to, the story; inevitable because we should sense all the time somewhere in the back of our minds where the story is headed. Scenes should be natural consequences of what has come before and they should be the natural causes of what follows.

Propp's 'Morphology of the Folktale'

This is one of the most celebrated (and still relevant) theories about the underlying, homogenous nature of all plots. In the 1920s, the Russian theorist Vladimir Propp looked at more than 100 folktales and drew up a chart, or 'morphology', of their basic elements. He first of all noted that there were only seven basic character roles:

Hero (a Seeker or a Victim)
Villain
Donor/Provider
Dispatcher
Helper
Princess
False hero

He then made a list of the thirty-one basic 'functions', as he called them. Not all the folktales included every single function, but the overall shape of all the tales remained the same. The functions are:

1. A member of the family leaves home or is absent.
2. A restriction of some kind is placed on the hero.
3. The hero violates that restriction.
4. The villain tries to find the hero.
5. The villain secures information about the hero.
6. The villain tries to trick the hero into trusting him.
7. The hero falls for it.
8. The villain hurts the hero's family or one of the family desperately lacks something.
9. This injury or lack comes to light and the hero must act.
10. The hero decides upon a course of action against the villain.
11. The hero leaves home.
12. The hero is tested in some way and, as a result, receives a magical agent or helper.
13. The hero reacts to the actions of the future donor.
14. The hero uses the magical agent or the helper aids him.
15. The hero is led to what he is looking for.
16. The hero fights the villain.
17. The hero is wounded or marked in some way.
18. The villain is defeated.
19. The injury or lack in function 8 is put right.
20. The hero returns.
21. The hero is pursued.
22. The hero is saved from this pursuit. (Propp notes that many of the folktales ended here.)
23. The hero returns home, unrecognized.
24. A false hero makes false claims.
25. A difficult task is set for the hero.
26. The task is accomplished.
27. The hero is recognized.
28. The false hero or villain is exposed.
29. The hero is transformed in some way.
30. The villain is punished.
31. The hero is married and/or crowned.

What is remarkable about Propp's morphology is how well it can be applied to all kinds of story from any period. Take the fourteenth-century Middle English alliterative romance *Sir Gawain and the Green Knight* as an example, looking at a synopsis of its plot in Proppian terms.

On New Year's Day in Camelot, King Arthur's court is feasting and exchanging gifts. A large green knight armed with an axe enters the hall and proposes a game. He asks for someone in the court to strike him once with his axe, on condition that the Green Knight will return the blow one year and one day later (4). Sir Gawain, the youngest of Arthur's knights and nephew to the king, accepts the challenge (5) (6) (7). He severs the giant's head in one stroke, expecting him to die. The Green Knight, however, picks up his head, reminds Gawain to meet him at the Green Chapel in a year and a day (New Year's Day the next year) and rides away (8) (9) (10).

As the date approaches Sir Gawain sets off to find the Green Chapel and complete his bargain (11). His long journey leads him to a beautiful castle where he meets Bertilak de Hautdesert, the lord of the castle, and his beautiful wife (12); both are pleased to have such a renowned guest. Gawain tells them of his New Year's appointment at the Green Chapel and says that he must continue his search as he only has a few days remaining. Bertilak laughs and explains that the Green Chapel is less than two miles away and proposes that Gawain stay at the castle (13).

Before going hunting the next day, Bertilak proposes a bargain to Gawain: he will give Gawain whatever he catches, on condition that Gawain give him whatever he might gain during the day. Gawain accepts. After Bertilak leaves, the lady of the castle, Lady Bertilak, visits Gawain's bedroom to seduce him. Despite her best efforts, however, he yields nothing but a single kiss. When Bertilak returns and gives Gawain the deer he has killed, his guest responds by returning the lady's kiss to Bertilak, without divulging its source. The next day, the lady comes again, Gawain dodges her advances, and there is a similar exchange of a hunted boar for two kisses. She comes once more on the third morning, and Gawain accepts from her a green silk girdle, which the lady promises will keep him from all physical harm. They exchange three kisses. That evening, Bertilak returns with a fox, which he exchanges with Gawain for the three kisses. Gawain keeps the girdle, however (14).

The next day, Gawain leaves for the Green Chapel with the girdle. He finds the Green Knight at the chapel sharpening an axe (15), and, as arranged, bends over to receive his blow (16). The Green Knight swings to behead Gawain, but holds back twice, only striking softly on the third swing, causing a small scar on his neck (17). The Green Knight then reveals himself to be the lord of the castle, Bertilak de Hautdesert (18), and explains that the entire game was arranged by Morgan le Fay, Arthur's enemy. Gawain is at first ashamed and upset, but the two men part on cordial terms (19) and Gawain returns to Camelot (20), wearing the girdle in shame as a token of his failure to keep his promise with Bertilak (21). Arthur decrees that all his knights should henceforth wear a green sash in recognition of Gawain's adventure (22).

Similarly, the first Star Wars film trilogy could easily be mapped by Propp's morphology, with the basic character roles as:

Hero: Luke Skywalker
Villain: Darth Vader
Donor: Obi Wan Kenobi (Provider = the Force)
Dispatcher: Luke's Uncle
Helper: Hans Solo/Chewbacca/Yoda
Princess: Leia

Of course, I'm not suggesting that anyone should slavishly follow Propp's schema, but it is an invaluable and illuminating way to see how a plot works in practice, from the inside.

Aristotle's 'Ars Poetica'

The first known person to attempt a literary analysis of narrative and what constitutes story and plot, however, was Aristotle (384–322 BC) and was published under the title *Ars Poetica*. This is the ur-text, the first and foremost piece of work for all Western thought and writing on narrative that followed. In it, Aristotle, too, differentiated between 'plot' and 'story', which he termed *mythos* and *logos* respectively, defining plot as 'the ordered arrangement of the incidents'. Many other terms and ideas Aristotle wrote about (particularly in Chapters 6–18) have entered the language and are still in common use today. In Chapter 6, for example, he separates out the basic elements of tragic drama into plot, character, diction, thought, spectacle and song. 'Of these elements,' he says, 'the most important is the plot, the ordering of incidents; for tragedy is a representation, not of men, but of action and life . . .' In this chapter, he also formulates what is probably his most famous idea, namely *catharsis*, which he defined as a kind of spiritual cleansing 'presented in the form of action, not narration; by means of pity and fear bringing about the purgation of such emotions'.

In the following chapter, he discusses the fact that plot must have 'a beginning, a middle and an end' and in the chapter after that, he states that the plot should promote the unity of action above character: 'The plot of a play, being the representation of an action, must present it as a unified whole . . .' In Chapter 10 he draws a distinction between 'simple' and 'complex' plots, saying that '. . . a discovery or a reversal . . . should develop out of the very structure of the plot, so that they are the inevitable or probable consequence of what has gone before, for there is a big difference between what happens as a result of something else and what merely happens after it'.

So much emphasis did Aristotle place on the importance of plot that, more than 2,000 years later, the crime writer Dorothy L. Sayers would say, after reading his *Poetics*, that '. . . what, in his heart of hearts, he desired was a good detective story . . .'. She went on to say, 'The *Poetics* remains the finest guide to the writing of such fiction that could be put . . . in the hands of an aspiring author.'

Aristotle's 'beginning, middle and end' is the blueprint for much of the narrative drama throughout Western history, right up to the present day, including Hollywood. One of the many gurus of screenwriting, Syd Field, drew a diagram based on Aristotle's *Poetics* to illustrate the basic three-act structure of most Hollywood movies.

ACT I	ACT II	ACT III
(set-up)	(conflict)	(pay-off)
0–30 mins	30–90 mins	90–120 mins

❶| ❷|

plot point   plot point

Field's term 'plot point' is just another name for Aristotle's 'discovery' or 'reversal', and refers to a key moment just before the end of an act that naturally brings about a partial closure of events in that act but also precipitates and propels the next act into play.

As an example of this three-act structure in operation, let's look at David Fincher's gloomy but extremely well-made thriller, *Se7en*, in which two homicide detectives work to catch the killer of an obese man who has been force-fed to death. Somerset, played by Morgan Freeman, is world weary and is due to retire in seven days; in contrast, Mills, played by Brad Pitt, is new to homicide and, despite the dreadfulness of his first case, refuses to relinquish his belief in humanity.

Told over seven days, the story hinges on whether or not the killer is, in fact, a serial killer. Somerset believes he is, citing the killer's obvious erudition and claiming that the victims will turn out to be paradigms of the seven deadly sins. Mills disagrees. If Somerset is right, he guesses the killer will strike again, and soon, so time is of the essence and both cops work round the clock to solve the case and make an arrest.

A scene-by-scene breakdown of *Se7en* illustrates particularly well how the plot points in Field's model exactly match the crucial moments in the plotting: whether or not the killer is a serial killer and discovering his identity.

ACT I (SET-UP)
- Somerset getting up/ready.
- Visits scene of crime – character revealment via colleague. Mills arrives.
- Slight conflict in street.
- Somerset in bed, metronome.
- Titles.

MONDAY
- Mills gets up/ready.
- Meets up with Somerset.
- First murder scene, Somerset pulls rank on Mills.
- Scene in car where Mills asks Somerset not to jerk him off.
- Forensic report.
- In office with Police Chief – conflict because Somerset thinks the murders will go on and on.

TUESDAY
- Newspaper headlines – death of Defence Attorney.
- District Attorney gives press conference.
- Mills at crime scene of second murder. (GREED)
- Somerset's office, Chief tells him of Defence Attorney's murder. Somerset at odds with city. Chief gives Somerset shards of plastic.

- Somerset goes back to first crime scene, note behind fridge.
- Police station. Somerset shows Chief and Mills Milton quote and photo (GLUTTONY). Serial killer confirmed. [**PLOT POINT 1**]
- Knife in dartboard.

ACT II (CONFLICT)

- Somerset in library intercut with Mills at home looking at photos.
- Somerset drops notes on Mills' desk.

WEDNESDAY

- Mills reads Dante in car.
- Enters Somerset's old office, hides Chaucer. Phone call, invitation to dinner.
- Somerset meets Tracey, she is go-between. Dinner. Ice is broken. Somerset and Mills talk about killings.
- They talk to wife of official. Painting upside down.
- Back to second crime scene.
- Fingerprint office. Corridor.

THURSDAY

- Asleep in corridor.
- Chief briefs cops on 'Victor'.
- Conversation in car about taking bullets/shooting people.
- Building stormed.
- Victor's room. (SLOTH)
- Waiting outside crime scene, Mills gets emotional. Disguised as a reporter, John Doe takes photos, Mills gives his name.
- Hospital doctor hints at atrocity.
- Tracey rings Somerset that night.

FRIDAY

- Somerset and Tracey in diner, conversation about kids.
- Police station, seven sins on blackboard. Mills out of his depth. Somerset gets idea about library from Mills.

- Library.
- Diner, informer arrives.
- Barber's. Somerset tells Mills about FBI's 'flagged' books.
- Car, they go through addresses.
- John Doe's apartment. Long chase, Doe lets Mills live. **[MIDPOINT]**
- Back to apartment, Mills breaks door down.
- Mills pays off witness.
- In room, they find photos. Phone call, photo of blonde.

SATURDAY

- Leather shop.
- Body in porn shop. (LUST)
- Interview rooms: Mills interviews porn shop owner; Somerset interviews client.
- Bar scene illustrating differences between Mills and Somerset.
- Mills gets into bed, tells Tracey he loves her.
- Somerset in bed, throws metronome across room. Throws knife in dartboard (three times).

SUNDAY

- Doe calls police – 'I've done it again.'
- Model's room (PRIDE), sleeping pills and phone glued to hand.
- Doe arrives in cab.
- Doe walks into police station. **[PLOT POINT 2]**
- Bloody fingerprints. Chief briefs Mills and Somerset – 'For the first time ever, you and I are in complete agreement.'

ACT III (PAY-OFF)

- Lawyer gives conditions. Unidentified blood on Doe's person.
- Shave off hair.
- Put on bulletproof vests.
- Doe brought to them.

- Car ride. Mills and Doe do all the talking, Somerset watches, listens and waits. Pylons, wide open space. They stop. Van arrives, Somerset meets it, box, Somerset runs. Doe tells Mills about his wife, that he envies his simple life (ENVY), about pregnancy. Mills shoots Doe. (WRATH)
- Mills taken away. Somerset says he will be 'around', quotes Hemingway in voice over.

Plotless narratives

'What I need today is not a book and movement forwards: I need a destiny, and grief as heavy as red corals.' – Viktor Shklovsky

Of course, not all narratives need, or indeed do, conform so strictly to the demands of 'plot'. I think of thrillers, and other examples of genre fiction that are highly plot-driven, as 'concave' narratives, in the sense that if you look at the structure, it is like looking through a lens that greatly concentrates the 'time of the thing told' (story) and the action. It follows that a 'convex' narrative would do the opposite, spreading the narration out, lengthening the time of the telling and slowing down the story's events (regardless of how long the story actually took to happen). Narratives looked at through a convex lens in this way usually pay much less attention to 'plot', preferring instead to dwell on deep interiority. As previously mentioned, such character-led narratives are usually labelled 'literary' fiction.

It's been said, for example, that the structure of *Waiting for Godot* is such that Beckett left himself free to lay down his pen at any moment. The same applies to the viewer and the reader, who are both free to walk away from the text at any moment without losing too much understanding of the play's themes or message (if there are any). This is because the play is without a discernible plot. Yes, characters come and go (although some cannot), and a few things happen, but the audience is largely none the wiser by the play's end than they were at the beginning.

Mike Leigh's *Naked* and Mike Figgis' *Leaving Las Vegas* are other examples of texts that don't have a plot. Of course they are narratives, in the sense that it takes us a certain amount of time to follow the story, which takes time to happen, but they are not stories that are made up of a linked series of events. Instead, the events in the stories 'just happen', one after the other, depending on what the capricious main character spontaneously decides to do. They are 'episodic' narratives, more accurately labelled chamber pieces or character studies. The roots of such narratives go much further back, of course: the story of the Immobilized Man can be seen in existential literature (Jean-Paul Sartre's *Nausea* and Albert Camus' *The Outsider*, for example), further back to Knut Hamsun's Modernist novel, *Hunger*, and even further back than that, ultimately to the work of Fyodor Dostoyevsky.

Kinds of Story or Genre

'A dead myth is called allegory.' – Michel Tournier

According to the nineteenth-century Frenchman Georges Polti (in a book published in English in 1916), there are a total of thirty-six dramatic situations in all fiction, including such variants as 'Supplication', 'Vengeance of a crime', 'Fatal imprudence' and 'Conflict with a god'. Others say that there are actually only seven original classical or mythological stories, and that all others are merely variations of these themes. The seven are the stories of Achilles, Candide, Cinderella, Circe, Faust, Orpheus, Romeo and Juliet, and Tristan and Isolde. Still others say that all stories can be reduced down to two basic types: 'the hero leaves home' and 'a stranger comes to town'. Respectively, these are the 'quest' narrative and the 'siege' narrative. Finally, there are some who say that there are, in fact, only three stories: boy meets girl; boy loses girl; man hunts whale.

While such rigid and drastic classification may be interesting only as an exercise, it is certainly true that 'quest' and 'siege' narratives are actually very prevalent models that have been used throughout the history of literature. Homer's *Iliad*, for instance, is clearly a 'siege' narrative, and his *Odyssey* is a 'quest'. These works are thought to have been written in the ninth century BC, which makes them the oldest extant works in European literature. *Sir Gawain and the Green Knight*, written in the fourteenth century, is most definitely a quest narrative, as are *Tom Jones, Jane Eyre, Star Trek* and *Finding Nemo* to name but a few. Typical siege narratives include *Hamlet, Hunger, Zulu* and *High Noon*.

These prototype stories are repeated endlessly. Take the film *Pretty Woman*, for example. What is the story? A rich businessman hires a prostitute, he falls in love with her and she is transformed into a beautiful woman. Does the 'rags to riches' storyline sound familiar? It should do, as the film is clearly a version of the Cinderella story. The stories of many very old myths and fairytales have been retold in this way throughout time. The story of Achilles, with his famously vulnerable heel, is retold as *Superman*, whose only source of weakness is exposure to Kryptonite; the deluded but chivalrous Don Quixote is reincarnated in the character of Alvin Straight who sets off on a journey from Iowa to Wisconsin on his lawn mower in David Lynch's *The Straight Story*; Mephistopheles makes a reappearance in *Wall Street* as Gordon Gecko, who espouses the creed 'greed is good' and tries to persuade Bud Fox to sell his soul for money and power; Orpheus' doomed journey into the underworld to retrieve his lost love, Eurydice, is reproduced as Vincent Ward's *What Dreams May Come*; and 'star-crossed lovers' Romeo and Juliet find modern equivalents in Rose and Jack in *Titanic*.

The original stories in myths and fairytales such as these are like bits of glass found on a beach, worn down by time but continually thrown up by the sea. They are the detritus of literature, cropping up repeatedly throughout history precisely because they are sophisticated lessons in morality and conduct. These stories are our masterplots, the mythological structure of society, told to us in various guises from a very early age, there not just to entertain, but to educate, too. In his book *The Uses of Enchantment*, Bruno Bettelheim looks at the Jungian archetypes and Freudian theories underlying many of our best-known fairytales, arguing that the darkness in these stories actually helps children to come to terms with very adult notions such as death, betrayal, murder, etc. These stories prepare young children for adulthood and aid them to integrate themselves into the world.

The kinds of stories that show themselves to be most easily classifiable when reducing them to their elements are inevitably myths and fairytales because these are the stories that are the most plot-driven and that employ the most archetypal characters. But this doesn't mean that stories cannot cross genres. In his essay 'The Wings of Henry James', James Thurber recounts the evening in a New York bar when Dashiell Hammett revealed that he had taken his inspiration for *The Maltese Falcon* from Henry James' novel *The Wings of a Dove*. Looking at the novels closely, you begin to see the similarities: both novels feature fabulous fortunes – jewels and an inheritance respectively; both plots revolve around a swindle; Kate Croy and Brigid O'Shaughnessy both lose their lovers. Miles Archer in *The Maltese Falcon* was named after Isabel in James' *The Portrait of a Lady* and Mr Cairo was so called because James had originally decided to use Cairo, not Venice, as one of the main settings in *The Wings of a Dove*. Or perhaps, as Thurber says, it is all just 'one of those rococo coincidences'.

As an aid to writing fiction, such reductive categorization is, ultimately, a hindrance rather than a help. It is true that plot is the genetic code of a text, but, just as human beings who share the same DNA are obviously and wildly different from each other, so books that show their common lineage are also peculiarly and stubbornly individual. Thank goodness for that. It is useful to see how stories can be categorized, but a novel isn't a machine that can be built simply by following a blueprint of a particular genre and assembling its elements. The spark, the seed, the *donnée*, will be missing, for a novel, unlike a machine, is greater than the sum of its parts. There are very many stories that follow more or less the same plot, but it is the writer's task to create stories, not copy plots. Stories these days might not be particularly unique, but they can still be genuine.

Character

'Outside in'
> 'He sees the world not as a writer might see it but as one of his characters might.' – James Wood on Chekhov

For many writers, character is the holy grail. But what is character? A friend once said that idiosyncrasy is the mother of all character and description the father, which is as good a definition as I've ever heard. When it comes to writing fiction, answering this question has provoked more anguish, debate and uncertainty than any other. It seems such a difficult task, one which has no obvious start or end point. It seems impossible to achieve without recourse to magic or voodoo. So, just how does a character on paper become a living, breathing citizen, walking and talking and acting in the world?

One ruse is to start from the 'outside in', as it were, to start with a few basic biographical details, such as age, star sign, occupation, interests. When I was doing my creative writing MA, my peers and I used questionnaires for characters, listing these basic details but also going into much greater detail about their habits, peccadilloes, distinguishing features and political views. Another trick to get started is to make a list of the first ten objects that come to mind and create a character out of as many of them as possible. It might seem like a trivial exercise, but you can tell a lot about someone by what they have on their person or at home.

In his collection of stories about Vietnam, *The Things They Carried*, Tim O'Brien starts by listing the things he and his fellow soldiers carried through necessity, things that comment very eloquently on the dangers, reduced circumstances and boredom of life as a grunt, and that make immediately apparent the differences between the men:

> P-38 can openers, pocket knives, heat tabs, wristwatches, dog tags, mosquito repellent, chewing gum, candy, cigarettes, salt tablets, packets of Kool-Aid, lighters, matches, sewing kits, Military Payment Certificates, C rations, and two or three canteens of water. Together, these items weighed between 15 and 20 pounds, depending on a man's habits or rate of metabolism. Henry Dobbins, who was a big man, carried extra rations; he was especially fond of canned peaches in heavy syrup over pound cake. Dave Jensen, who practiced field hygiene, carried a toothbrush, dental floss, and several hotel-sized bars of soap he'd stolen on R&R in Sydney. Ted Lavender, who was scared, carried tranquilizers until he was shot in the head outside the village of Than Khe in mid-April.

Another approach to character is via their name. Consider 'Luke Skywalker'. The first thing you notice about the name is how regal it sounds – a man who walks in the sky – which is perfectly fitting as he discovers during the course of *Star Wars* that he is indeed a prince. But there are other qualities about the name that comment on his character. Luke was an apostle, for instance, and the biblical name conjures ideas of honesty, uprightness, virtue and truth. Then there is the alliteration – those three plosive 'k' sounds are hard, abrupt, which implies that this man means business, that he is not to be messed with. The name 'Madame Bovary' summons up two key ideas: the book is called *Madame Bovary*, not *Emma Bovary*, and that 'Madame' tells us how aspirational and *petite bourgeoise* she is; also, the name 'Bovary' has a subliminal cow-like, bovine quality to it that comments on her nature. Finally, what does the name 'Lolita' tell us? Linguistically, it is very simple and musical – just three short vowel sounds – and it trills easily off the tongue. It is so simple that it could probably be recognized and uttered in any language. It also has a childlike, nursery rhyme quality to it, which, of course, is perfectly in keeping with the book's themes.

Another ploy is to describe, without mentioning a character by name, a character's home in such detail that we can gauge what kind of person lives there and what they do for a living. A variation of this approach would be to put a character into a landscape (a man in a rowing boat, fishing on a lake, for example) and write a two-page character sketch using the landscape and weather to intensify the reader's sense of what kind of person that character is. When carrying out exercises like this, however, bear in mind that it is important to restrict these details of characterization as much as possible, since it is the truth of the character we're interested in, not the facts, and there is a world of difference between 'character' and 'characterization'.

'Inside out'

> 'To be great, you must go from the inside out . . . Outside in
> is easy. It's journalism. Inside out is painful and dangerous.'
> – Robert McKee

These ruses and ploys are a good place to start for a novice writer, but they can soon seem mechanical and artificial. At some point, sooner or later, you are going to have to face up to the truth that, as a writer, it is absolutely vital that you know your characters in a way that goes beyond the circumstances of their day-to-day life, beyond their 'characterization'. It is a mistake to think that a means of paying the rent is an expression of the character's identity. No amount of mechanical character building can reach deep down into their innermost thoughts and feelings, to their very core, their quintessence.

In the best writing, it never takes much to summon and show a character's inner life – a brushstroke or two, nothing more. In Proust's *À la recherche du temps perdu*, for example, there is a famous moment when the narrator dips a madeleine into his cup of tea, an action that precipitates an instance of 'involuntary memory', a point in time when the narrator's past and present merge in his mind to produce a transcendental moment of epiphany and understanding about life, a unique sensory experience that had hitherto been unavailable to him and that he will never feel again. Although the impression is abstract and difficult to comprehend for the narrator, 'involuntary memory' is never brought on by anything other than the solid world of objects, it never recalls the indefinite article as abstraction does, and so its images are always concrete.

In his book, *Speak, Memory*, Nabokov talks about a moment as a young child when he was playing a game of matchsticks with a relative who was a soldier. He remembered the matches jumping in the air when the soldier got up from the sofa. That small, seemingly unimportant detail is what brings the memory to life. Years later, that same relative, by then very old, asks Nabokov for a light, a piece of information which surpasses its purely descriptive purpose and makes an elegant yet precise comment on the passage of time and how the child becomes father to the man. The devil is in the details.

To create an 'organic', wholly rounded, credible character in this way, you have to start thinking from the inside out, so to speak. That is all very well, but where on earth do you start? Part of the answer is to think beyond the page, as it were, and to look inside yourself. At some point, you will have to draw on your own inner being, the part of you normally kept hidden and out of reach. Ironically, if you want to express yourself, you have to give yourself away. If a moment from your life is needed for your story, then hand it over. Let your characters accrete gradually in the back of your mind, using your own experiences to help shape and form them.

Draw on your experiences with those around you, too. George Bernard Shaw defined a writer as someone who is 'half vivisector, half vampire'. Graham Greene talked about the necessity of having a 'splinter of ice' in the heart of a writer. If your book is going to have emotional honesty and veracity, you need to open and read other people's mail. But, even drawing on those around you, you will find that no fictional character is ever based on a single person – they are always composites. One way or another, actual biographical and autobiographical material will seep into your story whether you like it or not, to the point where what's real and what's invented become indistinguishable. Of your book, you can now say, 'None of this happened and it's all true.'

'Acting is doing'

'The purpose of living is an end, which is a kind of activity, not a quality . . .' – Aristotle

Aristotle's idea here is the fundamental rubric of character, the most primal, original, essential question for a writer – what are your characters going to *do*? Aristotle referred to action as *praxis*, from which we get the word 'practical.'

Think about someone you know who always talks about travelling to Marrakesh, or building a shed, or learning Japanese, but has never got round to it; now compare how you feel about someone who doesn't just talk up a task but gets on with it and does it. It is so much more impressive to see someone do what they say they will. As far as writing is concerned, the same applies – what your characters do in your story is far more revealing than what they say.

In an essay entitled 'Acting Is Doing', Sydney Pollack talks about how he directs actors. He says, 'The biggest mistake that's made in directing [actors] is talking about and working towards results instead of causes.' He goes on to say that, if he tells an actor to play a suspicious man, the actor will look for ways of playing 'suspicious'; if, however, he tells the actor to watch the other man's hand because he has a gun in his pocket, then that gives the actor something very specific to do. 'Characterization' is adjectival, but 'character' is a verb.

To paraphrase Aristotle, there is really no such thing as character, other than habitual action. The very fact of a character's existence precedes their essence. Watching people do things cuts to the quick of who they are much more quickly than any amount of words. And if there is no need for a character to do anything, then leave them thinking, fasting, waiting, until they are needed. As a character, all they can do is be as patient and as empty as possible. If characters become self-conscious, there is often an unattractive heaviness in the text, a kind of 'gravity' that burdens it, whereas what you are looking for is a kind of 'grace'. In the story, it's not what happens to them that's important, but how they react to it. A character's true fight within themselves is against this gravity, and the instrument of this fight is the idea of work, a project, a task. 'What are you *doing*?' Pollack writes. 'Acting is *doing*. Doing. Doing.'

Desire

> 'There's no such thing as adventure and romance. There's
> only trouble and desire.' – Hal Hartley

'Motivation' is an overused, jargony word, but it is true that characters have to do things for a reason. What do they want? The boy? The girl? The whale? Desire is wanting to have something, and wanting it badly. All character motivation stems from the difference between what a character has and what they want. If a character wants to become rich, for instance, it is a good idea to rob them first. Put obstacles in their path in order to make it difficult for them to achieve their goals – not impossible, just difficult. If a character brings about their success as a result of their own efforts in the face of great adversity, the reader will feel that success far more keenly than if it 'just happens' to come his or her way. The difference between what a character has and what they want is the basis for conflict and there is no story without conflict.

Identification

If desire is wanting to have something, then identification is wanting to be like someone. Such identification is the prime motivating factor in many psychological novels, or novels that delve deeply into human behaviour. A psychoanalytic theory called Object Relations states that psychological well-being is, for the most part, a matter of developing a capacity for healthy mental 'representation', which is important because it allows the person to mark out boundaries between self and the world. Neurotic representation, however, erects excessive representational boundaries between self and the world, ones that are designed to protect a vulnerable self. Such mental representations replace the actual world with private representations that are exaggeratedly developed and highly articulated, but which have no bearing on reality.

Ian McEwan's novel *Enduring Love* is just such a

'neurotic representation'. The opening, a *tour de force* of suspense (one of McEwan's signatures), involves a dramatic and tragic ballooning accident in which one man dies. Present at the accident is Joe Rose and a bystander, Jed Parry. Joe and Jed exchange looks. Unknown to Joe, though, is the fact that Jed suffers from de Clerambault's Syndrome, an obsessive disorder that causes the sufferer to believe mistakenly that someone else is in love with him or her. Delusional and dangerous, Jed gradually wreaks havoc in Joe's life, testing the limits of his rationale and driving him to the brink of murder and madness.

Choice

> 'Character is that which reveals personal choice, the kinds of things a man chooses or rejects when that is not obvious.'
> – Aristotle

If the origin of action is a character's desire put into practice, then it follows that the decisions a character makes regarding what he or she does (or does not do) reveal most about their character. Self-knowledge isn't only about knowing who you are, it's also about making good choices for yourself. If you continue to make the same mistakes when faced with the same dilemma, you have not learned your lesson and you have therefore not changed. Good judgement comes from experience, but experience comes from poor judgement. Aristotle's term for character was *ethos*, from which we get the word 'ethical'.

One of your jobs as a writer is to send your characters out into a story where you can shower them with circumstance, events and predicaments to see what happens, but it is only by forcing characters into difficult situations that you will see their true colours. Character is most revealed when the going gets tough. This is what Hemingway meant when he defined the 'courage' he saw in wartime as 'grace under pressure'.

'Suffering is inevitable, but misery is a choice.' – Christopher Reeve

As we have discussed, good characterization centres on 'doing', not 'being', on activity, not passivity, but a character can reveal themselves just as much by what they choose not to do. Self-knowledge is about making the right decisions at the right time, but it is also the case that, even though we have all the facts in front of us and know what we should do, we sometimes don't make a choice at all. Freud talked a great deal about this propensity for refusal, or denial. He wrote that when a person abolishes something internally, it will always return from the outside in the form of a delusion.

In Victor Hugo's novel, *Les Misérables*, for example, the policeman Javert has an obsessive desire to imprison Valjean, even though Valjean is, by the time Javert meets him, a reformed convict. For most of the novel, Javert relentlessly hunts and tracks Valjean down, only to let him slip through his fingers. Years later, during the Paris uprising of 1832, Valjean saves Javert's life, but Javert cannot cope with the mercy shown to him by Valjean and throws himself into the Seine. Despite Valjean's most profound efforts to better himself and contribute to society, he is continually hounded and persecuted by Javert. At the key dramatic moment, despite having every reason in the world to see him die, Valjean shows Javert the clemency that Javert has always denied Valjean, who actually deserves it much more. The illusion of occupying the high moral ground was, in reality, a delusion, and this realization is what forces Javert to hurl himself into the river.

It is interesting to note that Hugo found inspiration for his novel in the story of real-life criminal/policeman François Eugène Vidocq, and split his personality into the two main characters for his novel. They are two sides of the same coin, a symbiotic flow of guilt and 'justice', moral enterprise and stagnation, optimism and discrimination. Throughout the novel, Javert has many opportunities to end his extreme prejudice against Valjean, but chooses not to. As a result, his bigotry gradually transforms itself into a form of neurosis, and the moment he understands this exaggerated mental representation is the moment he dies.

Change

'People don't change, they only stand more nakedly revealed.' – Charles Olson

This idea of the 'exchange of guilt' is one of the most powerful transformations a character can go through. Whatever its kind, characters must undergo some degree of change for a story to have any kind of justification. This is the *sine qua non* of fiction, without which a story isn't really a story. Aristotle said, 'Change is giving form to matter.' By a story's end, characters should be transformed. They should have learned something about themselves which they hitherto did not know, self-knowledge that they did not possess. A narrative promises to take us through a set of screens, twisting and turning through strange lands and back out again, to the place where we began, but where everything is now utterly different. At the close of the narrative, we and the characters are the same people but now totally altered.

The existential situation

'Making a character "alive" means: getting to the bottom of his existential problem. Which in turn means: getting to the bottom of some situations, some motifs, even some words that shape him.' – Milan Kundera

In his book *The Art of the Novel*, Kundera writes that a novel is, in the final analysis, an 'existential enquiry', and that this enquiry is determined and driven by certain 'theme-words'.

For his novel, *The Unbearable Lightness of Being*, those theme-words are: weight; lightness; soul; body; the Grand March; shit; kitsch; compassion; vertigo; strength; weakness. Kundera, the ultra-modern novelist, is the ultimate puppeteer, introducing his characters like acquaintances and using them as mouthpieces for various ideas and anecdotes. He cannot get close to his characters; he says almost nothing about their physical appearance and there is no internal monologue in any of his novels. By maintaining this distance between implied author and text, Kundera gives himself room enough to explore felt subjectivity in the here-and-now. 'The novelist,' he says, 'is neither historian nor prophet: he is an explorer of existence.'

He does this partly by giving his characters very specific traits – indeed, you could argue that Kundera's characters are nothing *but* collections of character traits. These traits are used to signify the animation of characters and, if these attributes are used repeatedly, they become what James Wood refers to as a 'mnemonic leitmotif'. The more complex you wish to make a character, the larger their collection of several, varying traits. However, be wary of this approach. Kundera may treat his characters as marionettes and mouthpieces for his ideas, but he is also a master storyteller and an intellectual powerhouse. Beyond this point lie monsters. You can reduce characters to traits, but the most memorable fictional characters have a spark of vitality in them that cannot be accounted for by any number of character leitmotifs and theme-words, and that spark cannot ultimately come from anyone except the writer.

The spiritual aspect

'No man's wisdom goes beyond his experience.' – Tolstoy

One of the hardest tasks in building character is writing about people when they are on their own. Characters must have a physical aspect in a novel, interacting with other people and the world, but what are they like when they're sitting on their own in a room?

Tolstoy alluded to this obliquely in his suggestion that there are two possible ways forward in life from which people must choose. In his proposition, he says that one of these courses of action consists in giving a person a 'map' and pointing out the landmarks by which they must navigate their way. The success of finding their correct path depends entirely on the landscape, or the physical world, around them. The other method consists simply in giving the person a reading on a spiritual 'compass'. If the person keeps to this reading as they travel, not deviating in the slightest, they should find that they have stayed on the correct path.

The first type of path Tolstoy proposes makes use of external precepts, or rules: the person is given the lie of the land and they must move through the world in relation to what is around them. The second type relies more on an inner fortitude: the person is given a reading, a moral guidance, that they must take to heart and have faith in. If they keep to their word, they will inevitably reach their destination, despite whatever landmarks they may encounter along the way. This spiritual aspect is what characters can best show when they are sitting alone in a room, communicating with their inner self. Those moments when they think they are least observed by the world around them are the moments when they can reveal their innermost being. Wandering through fields of wheat, filled with spiritual conflict, Tolstoy's alter ego in *War and Peace*, Pierre Bezukhov, is a good example of such a character.

Deep interiority

In Knut Hamsun's novel *Hunger*, the starving main character (who remains nameless) wanders the streets of Oslo, encountering various strangers from whom he tries to scrounge a meal. His 'hunger' is not just for nourishment, however – he is drawn to make contact with the people he meets, but he also rejects them as soon as they show signs of responding to his requests. He craves, but ultimately cannot accept, help from his fellow man. In an article on the book, James Wood describes the character as an 'epistemological brawler', blaming his fate on God and vowing not to succumb to any sense he has of the divine world order. His mental representation of the world becomes increasingly unstable as his grip on reality loosens and paranoia sets in. Taken by themselves, his thought processes are perfectly logical, yet his mental and physical states deteriorate to an alarming degree and he is eventually forced to quit the city.

In the text, his character is represented, not as a continuous 'wave', but as a storm of interruptions. Hamsun, like Chekhov, was deeply suspicious of novels that presented characters as smooth and well-rounded, without flaws or foibles, lacking the angst they saw as a natural response to the brutal realities of modern life. Later, Virginia Woolf reacted in much the same way, stating that, for Edwardian novelists like Arnold Bennett, character was merely everything that could be described – houses, clothes, polite conversation. Woolf, however, felt passionately that character was everything that could *not* be described.

The ambition to show life as it really was and not as it perhaps should be – to create a deep interiority – was the aim of many Modernists, including Hamsun, Chekhov, Woolf and Henry James, who described this deep interiority as 'an immense sensibility, a kind of huge spider-web of the finest silken threads suspended in the chamber of consciousness, catching every air-borne particle in its tissue'.

One of our duties as writers is to acknowledge and explore the complexity of human life and experience, rather than merely subject characters to overdisciplined and organized plots, yet the idea of deep interiority is at odds with the demands of pure plot. Furthermore, it's the case that, since the Second World War, the Postmodern experiment has produced books that are much more concerned with connectivity and contingency than with deep characterization.

Plot versus character

'What is character but the determination of incident? What is incident but the illustration of character?' – Henry James

The discussion on what constitutes 'plot' and 'character' leads us to the inevitable and irresistible conclusion that they are, of course, yin and yang. Every moment that a character decides to do something (or not) changes the direction of the plot, while each event that happens (or not) in a plot has some impact and influence on the characters. You simply cannot have one without the other. Interiority arises out of action, which, in turn, shapes plot. As Scott Fitzgerald noted, 'Plot is character and character plot.'

A rich, rewarding novel is achieved by maintaining a balance between seeing a character 'acting' in the world and seeing them alone in a room. Creating character is arguably the greatest challenge facing any writer, irrespective of whether we are beginners or Booker prize winners.

Point of View

This is one of the most familiar terms in fiction and is self-explanatory: 'point of view' is the place from which we 'see' the story, the perceptual vantage point. The 'narrator' is what we call the person through whom we see the story, although they need not be a character in the story. The narrator is an agent adopted by the author to be the fictitious spokesperson in the text. As the term would suggest, point of view is all about distance and focus. Are you going to get up close to a character? Or will you 'shoot' everything in mid or long shot? Who is the centre of your story, and is the person you are going to focus on the same as your narrator? Deciding through whom we are going to see the story, and from where, is one of the most crucial decisions you will make as a writer.

'Suture'

Whatever the answers to these questions, 'suture' is the practice by which *any* point of view is established. The term refers to the process by which we are 'stitched into' the fictional world, or 'fabric', of a narrative. The process ensures that we are 'drawn into' the fictional world, taking up positions as 'subjects-within-the-text'. The most common way we are situated into a text is by suturing us into a position of identification with a particular character. In narrative cinema and fiction, this is achieved by shot/reverse-shot patterning, which shows us an image and then assigns the viewing of that image to a particular character in the text, thus ensuring identification with them.

Often, however, we may be sutured into the text to identify with the observer of the story, a character who is inside the fictional space but not part of the action. Nick Carraway in Scott Fitzgerald's *The Great Gatsby*, for instance, is the narrator of the story, but he is not a contributor to the plot; he is just the observer, the medium through which we see the story unfold. Because we are aligned with Carraway's point of view, we, too, are subjects-within-the-text and share his role as 'sleeping partner' in the text. It is interesting to note how insidious and effective this process is, rather like the narrative process itself – we hardly notice the 'seams' at all when a text is successfully suturing us into its fabric without our knowledge or consent.

When deciding on your point of view, you have five options to choose from: first-person, second-person (very rare indeed), single or multiple third-person, and omni-scient. The points of view from third-person singular and multiple, through to the omniscient, comprise a kind of sliding scale, rather than a series of disjunctions, as the focus of the story is diffused from one person to many and ultimately to an all-knowing, all-seeing entity in the sky.

First person

First-person point of view uses the pronoun 'I'. All the action is seen through the eyes of one person, with whom we stay in close proximity throughout the story, looking over their shoulder, as it were, as events unfold before our eyes (although it is important to note that the 'I' telling the story need not be telling their *own* story). This means that we see and hear only what the narrator can see and hear – our perspective is restricted and the action can never be opened out beyond this viewpoint. However, whatever perspective we might lose with a first-person viewpoint is more than compensated for by what we gain in intimacy. First-person narration is particularly suited to character studies and 'confessional' narratives.

J.D. Salinger's *Catcher in the Rye* and Sylvia Plath's *The Bell Jar* are both examples of confessional narratives, both written in the first person. Just think how different they would be in the third person – all their colour, flavour and depth of character would be lost. Writing his book in the first person allowed Salinger to climb into the mind of Holden Caulfield and conflate his voice with his view-point, so that we not only see what he sees, but we hear what he has to say about it. The greatest pleasure in Salinger's book is the voice of Holden Caulfield, a voice rendered with complete sympathy and authenticity.

William Faulkner's novel, *As I Lay Dying*, is an example of that rare thing, a novel written from multiple first-person viewpoints. Not only that, but each narrator's story is represented as stream-of-consciousness, occasionally making no concessions at all to standard speech or grammar. Although Faulkner helps us through this potential narrative minefield by naming each new narrator as they take up the narrative baton, so to speak, voice is even more essential here – apart from names, it is the only thing that differentiates between the series of 'I's, but the book is so skilfully written that we soon learn to distinguish between the fifteen different narrators. Graham Swift used a similar structure in his novel, *Last Orders*.

This use of multiple first-person narrators is also employed by Orhan Pamuk in his murder mystery, *My Name Is Red*, set in Turkey in the 1590s, among the world of the Sultan's miniaturists and illustrators. Here, Pamuk uses twenty different narrators, ten of which are the disembodied 'voices' of the colours in the exquisite illuminations painted by the leading characters – hence the title *My Name is Red*. Nine of the narrators are the illustrators themselves, of which the murderer is one. The final narrator is the voice of the murdered man himself, bitterly recounting his tale of woe and imploring anyone who may be listening to avenge his death.

Indeed, first-person point of view has a long tradition in murder mysteries in particular, and crime fiction in general, starting with Wilkie Collins' *The Moonstone* (1868), which is written as a series of first-person testimonies and is generally considered the first detective novel published in the UK. In the text, the detective is there *in praesentia* for the reader and so the reader can only know what the detective knows. We go over the same ground as the criminal (and the author), picking up clues and following the trail. If the investigator follows a red herring and makes a wrong turn in his case, so do we. First-person narration can be a very effective conjuring act, making it easy for the author to spring surprises on the detective (and us) and keep suspense levels high.

First-person perspective is also ideal for creating unreliable narrators. In Agatha Christie's *The Murder of Roger Ackroyd*, for example, we see events unfold through the eyes of the village doctor as he helps Hercule Poirot to investigate the murder of the eponymous victim. There are several plausible suspects but, in the end, Poirot reveals the murderer as the doctor himself. It is an odd, unsettling moment when Poirot points the finger at him and, by default, at us, too. This powerful, shocking ending forces us to re-evaluate everything the doctor has told us, and we begin to see the details he has omitted and the gaps in time when he must have been 'abroad', committing the crimes. It is a wonderful example of the ultimate confidence trick – we feel simultaneously collared and hoodwinked.

Third person – single

A single, third-person viewpoint can seem remarkably similar to the first-person point of view, albeit a little cooler, more distant. J.M. Coetzee's *Disgrace* is a good example of a novel that is written in the third person, but feels as though it is in the first. A large part of this effect is created by the use of the present tense, which brings an acute sense of immediacy to proceedings. Not only that, but the present tense Coetzee uses is the 'present perfect' – 'to have gone', for example. The first line of the book is: 'For a man of his age, fifty-two, divorced, he has, to his mind, solved the problem of sex rather well.' If we had used the 'simple past' tense here ('had'), the impression would have been that the narrator had some kind of vantage point beyond the closed events of the story. Keeping to the present perfect, however, gets us into the mind of the character and tells us that the ending of the story is not yet known, that everything that happens is contingent and the outcome provisional.

In the Coetzee sentence, if you were to replace the third person with the first, the meaning of the sentence would be kept, illustrating again how close first- and third-person narratives can be. But this is the exception, not the rule. If you have a sad story to tell (and Coetzee's story is very sad indeed), presenting it in the third person will nearly always render it slightly less intense. As similar as first- and single third-person points of view may initially appear, however, they are not completely interchangeable. It is a mistake to think than you can simply change the first-person pronoun 'I' to the third-person pronoun 'he' or 'she' and maintain perfect narrative clarity and comprehension. Occasionally, it works, but it is usually not possible to make a simple transition from first to third person. Try it for yourself: take a passage of writing, change the point of view from first to third as you read, or *vice versa*, and see what happens.

Third person – multiple

The clearest advantage of a multiple third-person viewpoint is that the narrator can move into the hearts and minds of more than one character, thus opening the story out considerably. What we gain in perspective with this point of view, however, we lose in intimacy. Because of this increase in perspective, this kind of viewpoint is particularly (but not exclusively) suited to writing that needs an impersonal, broad canvas on which to work. Establishing shots and wide-angle viewpoints – these are devices typical of more plot-driven stories, such as thrillers, epics and historical narratives. Scenes are rendered much more 'flatly', in long shot, so that the action may unfold without narratorial comment. If an intimate first-person narrative is written in a minor key, a multiple third-person epic is all crashing major chords.

Thrillers using this panoramic point of view can flit between characters and locations, showing us how they all connect in their own way to the central story and to each other. This can generate a great deal of suspense because we know, even if they don't, what is likely to happen to certain characters. Rather than springing surprises on us, this form of narrative tension is ratcheted up by us seeing our hero walk upstairs and knowing that there is a man behind the door holding a gun. This kind of viewpoint, where the reader or viewer has more information than any of the characters, is called 'dramatic irony'.

The suspense in Hitchcock's films works on this principle. A man sits on a bus with a ticking bomb in his bag. He gets off and places it under a table in a café and leaves. We see the people drinking tea and chatting, unaware that the bomb is about to go off any second. The tension mounts, we close in on some faces, laughing, talking, and then – *kaboom!* We know what is going to happen but, unable to communicate this information to the character, we can hardly bear the anticipation. So skilful is Hitchcock in building this kind of tension that most people don't realize just how heavily (but insidiously) they are being manipulated.

The downside to this viewpoint, however, is that, if it is not done well, the constant switching from character to character, location to location, can slacken tension. Switching points of view has to be done very carefully if it is to serve the story and keep up the pace. It is a tricky structure to use and very hard to get right.

Omniscient

> 'The author in his book must be like God in the universe: everywhere present and nowhere visible.' – Flaubert

The omniscient viewpoint is the classic, god-like view on the world beloved of nineteenth-century novelists. All-seeing and all-knowing, the narrator is free and unfettered, able to range over huge distances and penetrate people's hearts and minds. The narrator here acts as a highly polished mirror, reflecting everything it sees and refraining from filtering anything through its own consciousness. This point of view has fallen out of favour and is little used these days, although it can be used to dramatic effect. In Cormac McCarthy's novel, *The Crossing*, there is a moment when the narrator cuts from the close-up of a horse's eye to the sun rising over an enormous stretch of desert. The sudden switch from extreme close-up to furthest long shot is exhilarating.

'Versions' of the truth

Point of view can be used to show how different perspectives on the same set of events do not always corroborate each other. Akira Kurosawa's film *Rashomon* was the first Japanese film to be seen in the West and, in 1951, won the Golden Lion at the Venice Film Festival. Beautifully shot and edited, it is the story of the murder of a samurai warrior and the rape of his wife. The murder in the woods is witnessed by a woodcutter and a bandit is arrested for the crime. What follows is a series of testimonies, each conflicting with the others as they manipulate their own actions into appearing less blameworthy than they actually were.

The bandit claims that, after tying the samurai to a tree and raping his wife, he released the samurai and they fought a duel skilfully and honourably, which the bandit won. The wife, however, claims that, after she was raped, she released her husband and begged him to kill her, but that he was too cowardly to do so. She tried to kill herself with a dagger but failed, fainting and waking up later to find the dagger in her husband's chest. The woodcutter offers a different account again. In his version, the bandit raped the wife and then begged her to marry him, only to recant. Weeping, the wife released her husband, who told her coldly to stop crying. The woman railed at the two men, at the bandit for his capriciousness and brutality and at her husband for his lack of protection. In a rage, she provoked the two men into a duel. A pathetic struggle ensued, after which the samurai was killed while trying to flee.

In a final twist, we hear from the dead man himself, via a medium. In his account, the bandit did indeed ask the wife to run off with him after raping her. She accepted on condition that the bandit kill her husband. The bandit was shocked at such heartlessness and gave the samurai the choice of letting the woman go or killing her. The woman fled and the bandit released the samurai, at which point he killed himself with the dagger.

The point made elegantly and subtly in the film is that everyone has their own version of the truth and that none of these versions is ever the whole truth. We never discover what really happened because each witness to the murder paints their own involvement in it in the best possible light. In *Rashomon*, the term 'point of view' has a double meaning: it refers to a character's perceptual vantage point, but also to their opinion. Thus, the inherent semantic link between these two meanings of the term is made explicit and the text takes on a profound degree of ambiguity.

Dialogue

'If you're having trouble with dialogue between two people, bring in a third person, one who isn't supposed to be there.' – Alexander MacKendrick to Ronald Harwood

Think of a scene from a favourite book or film and the chances are that it will be memorable mainly because of its dialogue (which works in very similar ways, and on much the same level, in both fiction and film). There is nothing as fascinating or appealing to people as what they say to each other, and dialogue is the aspect of fiction or a film that can sparkle and scintillate to the greatest degree. But good dialogue is one of the hardest aspects of fiction to get right. If you listen to people talking in a café or on a bus, and transcribe it, you'll find it full of repetitions, slang, bad language, silences, *non sequiturs*, 'you knows', 'likes', etc., which is not at all interesting to read. One of the first things to learn about good dialogue is that it is an *impression* of how people really speak – an approximation, not a facsimile.

The second key point to remember is to keep dialogue down to the absolute minimum at all times. There should never be too much of it – action is always better, if possible. The temptation for novice writers is to write reams and reams of dialogue, expanding it to the point where any meaning it might have completely disappears, whereas what they should be doing is compressing the dialogue, keeping it down to the barest minimum so that meaning expands as much as possible. This will mean making it quite unrealistic, but dialogue is not 'real', it is an *intensification* of speech, so don't worry – the semantic 'leaps' between lines of dialogue can be much greater than you think.

Here are two excerpts from films. Which one do you think is an example of good dialogue and which bad? Why?

> 'You know, when I was a kid, I always thought I was gonna grow up to be a hero.'
> 'Well, it's too late now.'

> 'What did you expect from this?'
> 'I don't know – maybe some self-realization.'

In the first exchange, from *Butch Cassidy and the Sundance Kid* (written by William Goldman), we understand that the speakers know each other well, that there is a strong enough bond between them to allow for this kind of open banter. The dialogue is attractively warm and witty. The idealism and cynicism in the lines are 'markers' for the characters of Butch and Sundance, respectively, things that differentiate them and identify them as individuals. This rich exchange of words reveals character to us, and good dialogue should grow out of character and the story in this way.

In the second exchange, however, the connection between the speakers is not so clear and the dialogue is too 'on the nose', stating something rather than revealing it. In this sense, this exchange (from the film *Van Helsing*) is an example of poor dialogue because it is telling us something about the character instead of showing it.

Think of a scene from a film you saw or a book you read recently that contained a lot of dialogue and make a list of the functions you think the dialogue performed. Then add what else you think dialogue should do. How many of the following functions did the dialogue you looked at perform? It should:

1. Characterize the speaker, and perhaps the person addressed.
2. Be idiomatic, maintaining the individuality of the speaker, yet still blend with the story.
3. Reflect the speaker's mood.
4. Often reveal motivation, or attempt to hide motivation.
5. Show relationship of character to other characters.
6. Be connective; that is, grow out of the preceding speech and lead into the next.
7. Advance the action.
8. Sometimes carry information or exposition.
9. Often foreshadow what is to come.
10. Be clear and comprehensible to the audience.

In Michael Mann's *Collateral*, Max, a Los Angeles taxi driver played by Jamie Foxx, has unknowingly picked up an assassin, Vincent, played by Tom Cruise. Vincent has hired Max for the night because he has to make several stops. At the first of these stops, Max is waiting for Vincent in an alleyway when a body falls on the roof of his cab. Max looks on aghast. Vincent returns and pulls a gun on him.

Here is an excerpt of dialogue from the film. As you read through the scene, tick off how many of the above criteria the scene fulfils.

Vincent: We gotta make the best of it, improvise ... Darwin, shit happens, I-Ching, whatever – we gotta roll with it.
Max: I-Ching? What you're talking about, man? You threw a man out a window!
Vincent: I didn't throw him. He fell.
Max: But what did he do to you?
Vincent: Nothing. I only met him tonight.
Max: You just met him once and you kill him like that?
Vincent: What, I should only kill people after I get to know them?
Max: No, man ...
Vincent: Max, six billion people on the planet ... You're getting bent out of shape over one fat guy?
Max: Well, who was he?
Vincent: What do you care? Have you ever heard of Rwanda?
Max: Yes, I know Rwanda.
Vincent: Tens of thousands killed before sundown. Nobody's killed people that fast since Nagasaki and Hiroshima. Did you bat an eye, Max? Did you join Amnesty International, Oxfam, Save The Whale, Greenpeace or something?
Max: No.
Vincent: But I off one fat Angeleno and you throw a hissy fit.

How many of the functions did you tick? In the scene, Vincent and Max are obviously at odds with each other (5); Max is horrified and Vincent is aggressive (3); Vincent is shown to be purposeful, yet can adapt to changing situations (1); the words 'Darwin, shit happens, I-Ching, whatever' are an idiomatic 'marker' of Vincent's personality (2); the plot – that Vincent forces Max to drive him around Los Angeles during the course of one night – is advanced (7). In addition, the dialogue in the scene carries a certain amount of information, it foreshadows what is to come, it is connective, and is clear and comprehensible to the audience. The only function it doesn't perform is number 4, because Max doesn't yet know that Vincent is an assassin, a fact that Vincent goes to great lengths to keep from him.

This passage is an excellent illustration of how many things good dialogue can do at any one time. Dialogue should not only snap, crackle and pop on the page, but, although it might not be able to do all of them, it should perform as many of these functions as possible *at the same time*.

Subtext

When writing dialogue, always be thinking about the subtext of what characters say, the meaning behind their words. There's a great scene in Woody Allen's *Annie Hall* when Annie (played by Diane Keaton) and Alvy (played by Allen himself) are both in therapy and the true meaning of what they say pops up on screen as subtitles. How does what a character says relate to what they do, or what they know, or don't know? Making characters simply say what they mean will usually lead to flat and dull dialogue, but putting a façade on a character, so that we have to dig behind what they say to find out what they really mean, is far more intriguing and involving for the reader.

Not only can characters not mean what they say, they might not actually be listening to another person at all. In life, people often don't really listen to their friend, lover or relative, because they are too busy thinking about what they want to say and are merely waiting for the opportunity to do so. Having your characters talk to each other like a game of ping pong can lead to dreary and two-dimensional dialogue, but having them talking at cross-purposes like this, addressing their own issues instead of the other person's, is an effective way of revealing character and showing the conflict between them.

'Voice'

Many novice writers are told that one of the most vital things for a writer to do is 'find your voice', as if you had once lost it. Without your 'voice', they say, you are indistinct as a writer, you have no signature. 'Voice' is one of the biggest myths in writing and has caused more loss of heart than anything else for writers just starting out. You can no more 'find' your voice than you can relax when told to. Telling someone to relax is the thing least likely to make them do so.

Rather, when novice writers are told that they have to find their 'voice', what they are in fact being told is that it may take some time before they grow sufficiently in confidence to let whatever inherent ability they may have to shine through. What we mean when we say a writer has 'found their voice' is that their storytelling abilities and prose style have reached some kind of zenith in textual terms. The 'implied author' in their texts is some kind of version of their writing 'voice'.

In narratological terms, what this misunderstood term is actually referring to is the tone of voice the narrator speaks in, the quality of language in their report. It refers to the speech patterns, 'marker' phrases, linguistic tics and idiosyncrasies, etc. used by the author to reveal the personality of the narrator. So, while some may say that 'voice' refers to the author's fluency of expression or writing style, it is actually more about how the narrator *sounds*.

A caveat from the outset: although they are inextricably

entwined, 'voice' is *not* the same thing as point of view and the two terms should not be used interchangeably. Point of view is the perceptual vantage point from which the story is told, it is what you *see*; 'voice', on the other hand, is what you *hear*. The crucial point to remember is that perspective and expression do not necessarily come from the same person. As with the differences between 'story' and 'plot', this is an issue that causes great confusion and frustration for new writers, so let's look at it in more detail.

In his book, *Story and Discourse*, Seymour Chatman posits four comments on the same, complete event:

> I felt myself fall down the hill.
> I saw Jack fall down the hill.
> Mary, poor dear, saw Jack fall down the hill.
> Jack fell down the hill.

Looking at the one event from these four perspectives, we can say with certainty that it is Jack who fell down the hill. The 'I' in the first sentence, then, is Jack, who is narrating his own story. In the second sentence, however, he is no longer the narrator, but we don't know who is. In the third sentence, the fact that Mary is the witness to Jack's fall is reported by a third party, so this clears up who the 'I' is in the second sentence – Mary. So Mary was present at the scene and she witnessed Jack's fall. In the second sentence, she is the narrator *and* a character in the story. In the third sentence, however, who is this third party who reported to us that Mary saw Jack fall? We don't know but, whoever it is, one thing is clear: in the third sentence, the point of view from which the story is told is assigned to a narrator who is *not* a character. Finally, in the fourth sentence, it is not clear at all who witnessed Jack's fall – the narrator is omniscient.

The aim of this example, Chatman says, is to demonstrate that 'perspective and ... expression need not be lodged in the same person'. The narrator in the third sentence was not present at the scene, but, in reporting the event, shows some sympathy ('poor dear'). It was not necessary for the narrator to show any feeling one way or the other in reporting the fact that Mary saw Jack's fall but, in addition to reporting the facts of the case, they chose to do so. Even in this brief example, this sympathy is what reveals the narrator's personality to us – it is the narrator's 'voice'.

To illustrate this point further, Chatman goes on to quote examples from three texts:

A few moments [later] he found himself on the stage amid the garish gas and the dim scenery. (From James Joyce's *A Portrait of the Artist as a Young Man*)

He shivered a little, and I beheld him rise slowly as if a steady hand from above had been pulling him out of the chair by the hair. (From Joseph Conrad's *Lord Jim*)

Coffin now. Got here before us, dead as he is. Horse looking round at it with his plume skewways. Dull eye: collar tight on his neck, pressing on a bloodvessel or something. (From Joyce's *Ulysses*)

In the first example, the perceptual vantage point is Stephen Dedalus', but he is not the narrator. We know this because, if Stephen Dedalus were the narrator, it would sound unnatural and implausible for him to pass judgement on how the stage seemed to him (the 'garish gas and dim scenery') at precisely the moment he stepped onto it. The pejorative adjectives here are the narrator's, not Stephen's, and they bring to light the 'voice' of the narrator.

In the second example, the 'I' is a character in the text and is the point of view from which we see the story (the narrator), so the perceptions are the character's. Despite the character perceiving the action in the first instance, however, the act of reporting it ('I beheld him rise . . .') places an implicit distance between the narrator-as-witness and the narrator-as-reporter. In both cases, though, the narrator's 'voice' is not made so apparent because the narration is purely descriptive of the action – there is no narratorial 'comment'.

The final example is a little less straightforward (as things always are in *Ulysses*). The narrator here is Leopold Bloom, so we are seeing things through his eyes, but the words he uses are so interior that we are not sure who exactly is speaking. The boundary between character and narrator is blurred here because narrator and character are so closely conflated. This is typical of stream-of-consciousness narration, in which the narrator is not 'mediating' so much as 'capturing' a character's thought processes. It is not as if Bloom is thinking to himself – the words come from a deeper place than that – it's almost as though there is no narrator at all (though of course there is).

To illustrate the idea of 'voice' for yourself, there is a well-known writing exercise, suggested by John Gardner, in which the writer must describe a barn as seen by a person whose son has just been killed in a war. The trick is that you are not allowed to mention that fact, so the writing becomes an exercise in pure 'voice' as the building becomes imbued with the narrator's interior state. The writer then has to repeat the exercise, this time from the point of view of a person who is in love. But, again, you are not allowed to mention that fact. In both cases, the hidden agendas remain secret, and the barn becomes 'animated'.

Setting

'We go outside of ourselves because we do not know what it is like on the inside.' – Montaigne

It is easy to underestimate the importance of setting. Ideally, the setting of a novel should be as 'present' as any of the characters. The reader should be able to 'see' the background of a novel without even realizing it, for without a strong sense of setting, the fictional world of a novel will seem thin and underdeveloped and characters will appear unanchored, rootless. Just imagine if *Ulysses* hadn't been set in Dublin, if Franz Kafka's *The Trial* wasn't set in Prague, Emily Brontë's *Wuthering Heights* without the North York moors, Hardy's work without Wessex, or Faulkner's without Yoknapatawpha County – all these places are 'local' to these writers and their books would be unthinkable without this strong sense of place.

It is clearly in your favour if the setting of your novel is familiar to you, but many writers starting out may opt not to write about the place they are most familiar with. In an article on this subject, David Almond writes how, for years as a writer, he completely avoided writing about the place in which he grew up – Tyneside – setting his novels instead 'in the garden suburbs of Surrey, on the surface of Mars, in the Australian outback'. He goes on to describe the Sunday market that was held on Newcastle's quayside, to which his grandfather used to take him. He says, 'There were fortune-tellers, quacks, masseurs, strongmen, almanac-sellers, acrobats, racing tipsters, buskers, magicians, card-sharps . . .' In particular, he remembers a strongman who 'stabbed himself with needles, whacked himself with metal bars, broke free from straight-jackets and chains' and who afterwards would sneer and say, 'Pay! Get yer money out and pay!' When Almond started writing a book about an escapologist, he avoided using any of these childhood memories and produced a book that was 'strange . . . long-winded and aimless'. Only when he decided to base his main character on the man from the quayside market did the book come to life.

Knowing your hometown so intimately and at such a

profound level gives a great deal of creative freedom. It is only when something is absorbed so completely, when it becomes an ineffable part of your being, that you can play so freely with it. The details are not 'on your mind', waiting to be employed, but deep down inside, from where they can be summoned at will. Even if you do know the setting for your novel very well, however, it is still a good idea to do some research into the area: locally produced guide books, council street plans, local libraries are all great sources of information and detail. Walking around an area to get a sense of the place is vital, too – examining architecture, seeing how streets connect, how times have changed.

Obviously, you will have to do a huge amount of research if you are not familiar with a particular setting, but be careful not to let this research overwhelm your writing. It is the 'truth' of a place you're after, not the conveyance of information. You need to ensure the details of your setting are accurate, but much more important is communicating a distinct, direct impression of its environment. The aim is to rebuild a place in the reader's mind, not merely describe it. Use specific nouns whenever possible – nouns identify a place, verbs energize it and adjectives colour it. Is a house Georgian or Victorian, is the tree an ash or an oak, is the flower an aster or a daisy, exactly what shade of red? The reader will be situated and rooted in your setting if you provide them with such particular features. They act as portals into the imagination for the reader. As with creating a convincing character, less is more – a detail that is eye-catching and unique to that place will recreate a sense of place better than any amount of description.

'The environment can act on the subject only to the extent that they comprehend it; that it transforms it into a situation. Hence no objective description of this environment could be of any use to us.' – Sartre

As this quote shows, Sartre suggests making no separation between self and world when describing setting. In this psychological landscape (*le paysage intérieur*), everything connects to, and is an expression of, a state of mind. This is one of the defining characteristics of existential literature, which sought to articulate a character's sentient self through the landscape around them. This is a kind of demented version of Ruskin's 'pathetic fallacy' (in which inanimate natural objects are infused with human feeling), but it is a version of it that is twisted through the prism of 'existence', and weighed down with torpor.

Think of Mersault, in Camus' *The Outsider*, as he steps on to the white sand beach: 'The sun was crashing down on to the sea and the sand and shattering into little pieces.' When he is handed the gun, the sun 'glinted off it' and 'the whole beach was reverberating in the sun and pressing against me from behind'. At the decisive moment, when Mersault is about to shoot the Arab, he says, 'All I could feel were the cymbals the sun was clashing against my forehead . . . The sea swept ashore a great breath of fire. The sky seemed to be splitting from end to end and raining down sheets of flame.' This example of Camus' famous 'white prose' is stripped down, connective and direct, and conveys emotion through landscape supremely well.

Think about the area you grew up in. What was it like? How big was your house? Was it terraced or detached? What was it like on the outside? Was it stuccoed or open-brickwork? Pebble-dash? Think back to your childhood bedroom and place yourself back in it as a child. Try to remember the size of it, the wallpaper, the furniture, the smells, the sounds in the house and from outside, too, and write about it. Now imagine yourself in bed, ill. Rewrite your description of the bedroom with that in mind. How does that detail affect the environment around you?

PART II: AID

5. The Role of the Narrator

'Tell me and I'll forget. Show me and I'll remember. Involve
me and I'll understand.' – Chinese proverb

The kind of role you assign your narrator is one of the two
most fundamental and crucial decisions you will make
when writing fiction (the other being the handling of the
passage of time). Are you going to allow your narrator to
do no more than 'record' the words and actions of your
characters? Or will you let them delve deeply into their
interior life? The decisions regarding how much you allow
your narrator to be involved in the telling of your story will
largely determine what kind of book you write.

In any reading and writing experience, there is a
complex set of relationships between the author, the narrator, the characters and the reader. As the writer, which of
these relationships do you wish to promote? For example,
if the author and narrator are 'one' with each other, you are
taking the reader into the realms of autobiography or
memoir. If, on the other hand, you wish to encourage a
rapport between the narrator and the reader, the narrator
may well address the reader directly, thus bypassing character (and therefore story) altogether. This can lead to a

certain playfulness on the narrator's part, depending on how sincere they wish to be. The narrator may, for instance, not be telling the truth, and so the reader gradually learns to mistrust their version of events, or perhaps they adopt an ironic tone with respect to the story they are telling.

If, however, you want the narrator and characters to be as closely aligned as possible, your narrator has a choice of either showing us directly what the characters say and do, or entering into their hearts and minds to tell us what they think and feel. In both cases, the narrator can be a 'transparent medium', largely invisible, but they can also make their presence felt in the narrative and play a large role in the telling of the story.

The Unreliable or Ironic Narrator

The first-person narrators in these kinds of texts are usually talking to themselves, or to the readers, just as much as they are telling a story. 'Unreliable' narrators are economical with the truth, to say the least, usually because they have something to hide or because they are in denial about some aspect of themselves. When reading texts narrated by characters we cannot trust, we must learn to read between the lines to seek the truth; we have to cast ourselves as detectives, picking up meaning 'behind' the narrator's account and putting together the real version of events for ourselves.

This is certainly the case with Humbert Humbert, the narrator in Nabokov's *Lolita*. During the course of the narrative, he repeatedly tries to make light of his 'predilection' and aims to paint as rosy a picture as possible of his road trip and eventual settlement with 12-year-old Dolores Haze (whose name he prettifies to 'Lolita'). Tarquin Winot, the narrator of John Lanchester's *The Debt to Pleasure*, is another such ironic, unreliable fantasist, who relishes the sound of his own voice as he hints at, but glosses over, the fact that he is a psychopath. Equally eccentric, and 'enchanting', is Erskine Flesching, the opera-singer-turned-murderer in Kym Lloyd's *Erskine's Box*.

All these books have very dark themes – paedophilia, matricide, castration – but their subject matter is made more palatable by the urbanity, intelligence and wit of their narrators. Speaking after the fact, the narrators of these stories have distanced themselves from their acts, a gap they fill with language that sparkles and shines, but flatters to deceive. They are detached from events, but they have in common a desire to be heard and, if not sympathized with, then at least understood. They are society's *outré* outcasts and therefore speak from the margins. These *tour de force* narratives are linguistic high-wire acts, but they are also confidence tricks, with their narrators continually attempting to pull the wool over our eyes.

Stenographer, Reporter or Interpreter

In third-person narration, things are slightly different. The fact that the narrator and the main character are the same person in first-person narratives is, by definition, not the case in third-person narratives. In spite of that, however, it is still possible to align narrator and character extremely closely together, and the degree to which the narrator aligns themselves with the character is set as a kind of 'sliding scale', ranging from remaining steadfastly outside the character's body to purposefully climbing inside their head and heart.

As with a court stenographer, one role the narrator can play is to act as nothing more than a medium through which we see directly for ourselves what the characters do and say. In this role, the narrator makes no attempt to tell us what the characters are thinking or feeling; the narration is merely a transcription. It is all about action and words, not moods or emotions. The important point here is that the narrator remains so 'invisible' in the text that the story seems as though it is being shown to us first hand, as it were – directly, without mediation.

There are certain kinds of writing that lend themselves particularly well to the role of narrator-as-stenographer. The 'hardboiled' crime stories written by Dashiell Hammett, for example, are stripped down to their bare bones of action and direct speech. The narrator in Hemingway's early fiction, too, is nowhere to be seen.

Further along the scale lies the moment when the narrator enters the body, and the view from which the story is told shifts to a point somewhere inside the character. Not only do they continue to show us what a character says and does, the narrator-as-reporter is now privy to his or her thoughts and emotions – all cognitive processes, in fact. As well as playing the role of a stenographer, the narrator now also acts as mind-reader, reporting to us what the character is thinking and feeling.

When the narrator tries to record a character's thoughts for an extended period, we label it 'interior monologue' and we say that the prose is written in 'free direct style' – 'direct' because it allows the narrator to 'quote' these thoughts as if they were direct speech, and 'free' because there are no 'tags' ('he said') or quotation marks. For example: 'It was unbearably hot in the room. I can't stand it here! She decided to leave.' The 'unspoken speech' of free direct style is rendered in the present tense and in the first person; if, however, you transfer it to the third person and set it in the past tense of reported speech, it is called 'free indirect style'. But the difference between free direct and indirect styles is more subtle and complicated than that.

The sentence ' "I will stay here tomorrow," she thought' is an example of direct 'speech', a report of which would be: 'She thought that she would stay the next day.' Free indirect style takes the past tense and third person of reported speech – 'she would stay' – and combines them with the time and place of direct speech – 'here tomorrow' – to come up with: 'She would stay here tomorrow.' This writing style is best summed up as a fusion of third-person point of view with first-person consciousness. The shift into the past tense in 'free indirect style' implies a shade more intervention by the narrator than with 'free direct style', but it is very much the case that 'free indirect style' still sounds more like a character 'speaking' than a narrator 'reporting'.

Flaubert was one of the great exponents of this style, called *le style indirect libre* in French. In the following example from *Madame Bovary*, the narrator records Emma Bovary's movements, but then mediates to us some questions she asks herself before recording another movement and some of her speech. These questions are the moment when the narrator is entering Emma's consciousness and showing us what she is thinking.

> She looked about her with the wish that the earth might crumble about her. Why not end it all? What restrained her? She was free. She advanced, looking at the paving stones, saying to herself, 'Come! come!'

Despite being an attempt at capturing the complexity of deep interiority, these forms – interior monologue, and free direct and indirect styles – still respect and preserve the standard grammatical and syntactical conventions of the language. 'Stream-of-consciousness', however, does not. The term (coined by Henry James' psychologist brother, William) refers to the attempt by the narrator, as the term implies, to capture not only the product of the thought process, but the process of thought itself. Stream-of-consciousness goes a step further into consciousness, in that it not only encapsulates cognitive processes, but also perceptions.

Seymour Chatman uses the example that, whereas it is perfectly normal to say to yourself, 'I must get milk and bread' while walking along a path, it is rare to say, 'That rose is red' when you pass a garden. The former is a verbalized thought, whereas the latter is something perceived. 'The latter,' Chatman says, 'is something "felt" rather than said.' As well as verbalized thought processes, it is exactly these perceptions that stream-of-consciousness also attempts to capture. In stream-of-consciousness, the narrator is so deeply embedded within the character that they are not there; their presence goes unnoticed. Stream-of-consciousness narrative is body language, but without the body.

Virginia Woolf and James Joyce were both great exponents of this technique. In the following example, 'dull eye' is something Bloom notices, but only somewhere deep in the back of his mind, not in the forward, cerebral part of his brain.

> Coffin now. Got here before us, dead as he is. Horse looking round at it with his plume skewways. Dull eye: collar tight on his neck, pressing on a bloodvessel or something. (from Joyce's *Ulysses*)

Both these roles that a narrator can play – narrator-as-stenographer, showing us directly what the characters say and do, narrator-as-reporter of what a character thinks and feels by means of interior monologue, free direct and indirect style – allow characters to shine through unmediated. They avoid offering retrospective understanding of what a character says and does, and they refuse to put their characters on the couch. The role of narrator-as-stenographer allows for pure action and description, set firmly in the external world, while stream-of-consciousness makes no apologies for wishing to explore the depths of character without comment or judgement.

110

Although narrators are frequently blurred with the thoughts of characters in interior monologue and free direct and indirect styles, there are times when the narrator separates themselves from character, yet still offers their own comments on a character's words, actions, thoughts or feelings. The narrator is now acting as narrator-as-interpreter, telling us, seemingly for our benefit, the real meaning or significance of those words, actions, thoughts or feelings. This is the instance when the narrator's role in the telling of the story is at its most visible in the narrative. These comments have little to do with story, adding instead an extra layer of narration.

This tendency is better known as that golden rule of writing: 'Show, don't tell.' This maxim, attributed to Henry James, refers to the role assigned to a narrator whereby they interject and comment on events, confirming to us what we have already seen for ourselves, or interrupting to announce what we are about to see for ourselves. For example: 'All day long she had felt an unease, a restlessness as she had never experienced before . . . 'Her grief was boundless'; and 'She was beside herself with excitement.'

The temptation for inexperienced writers is to try to 'bolster' a moment, to imbue it with portent, but rather than empowering the moment, this tendency impoverishes it. We must feel this unease, restlessness, grief and excitement for ourselves, not have the narrator tell us that it is so. We need to see these things first-hand, not hear about them second-hand.

One of the ways you can do this is by having characters perform actions that express these feelings. A way of conveying grief is to show a character crying, which is of course obvious, but still preferable to having the narrator merely tell us, 'Her grief was boundless.' Restlessness is a far subtler mood to evoke, but you could perhaps convey it by showing a character going for a very long walk and commenting on the landscape he or she sees around them. Mersault's walk on the beach in Camus' *The Outsider* is a very good example of the reader being shown Mersault's state of mind rather than having the narrator tell us.

If you rely on the narrator to tell us what the character is feeling or thinking, we have no choice but to take it on trust and we are kept at arm's length from the characters and the story. Remove the narrator from the process of telling your story, however, and now the story unfolds naturally in the mind of the reader, drawing them in as they watch and listen to the words and actions of the characters themselves. Such 'telling' is to be avoided whenever possible. Less really is more.

'The fundamental accuracy of statement is the one true morality.' – Ezra Pound

6. Creating Obstacles for Characters

'To get out, go in deeper.' – Roland Barthes

The Idea of Conflict

If plot is the engine of a narrative, its heart, then the idea of conflict is the heartbeat. Put simply, without conflict there is no story. If the fact that a character will find success is never in doubt, there is no interest or involvement for the reader. The gap between desire and its fulfilment is what drives the story and keeps us glued to the page.

For writers commencing on a novel for the first time, the idea of conflict is often overlooked. Very often in the case of inexperienced writers, when there is a change in a character's circumstances, this change is brought about extremely easily and without much opposition or many obstacles. Hey presto, just like that, the character has everything that they have always dreamed of and none of it has come about through their own hard work or at any cost to themselves. It is all too easy.

The effect of this is that the story feels thin and undeveloped, and there can often be a predictability to the story that turns it into an undemanding read. The main character might be exposed to tragedy, but the experience doesn't seem to run too deeply within them. They remain unmarked by events and unmoved by encounters. This makes the reader feel that your main character has no 'inner life', no depth. This is especially true when the character's main goal, the whole purpose for their being, has been built up over a significant amount of time, only to be dispatched in the blink of an eye. We are left feeling underwhelmed, to say the least.

Furthermore, if this lack of conflict within a character also occurs *between* all the characters in a novel, things can become very dull indeed. If the text is comprised solely of people being nice to each other, exchanging pleasantries, making arrangements, etc., the reader will become bored stiff and will switch off.

In order to avoid all of this, you need to put obstacles in the character's path to make life difficult for them. Their progress cannot be too smooth, so put things in their way in order to prevent them from getting what they want. A locked door, a choice between two lovers, a mistake rued. Each obstacle presents a character with a psychological threshold and, when they reach and pass through that threshold, they are transformed into a different person.

The trick is to make these obstacles seem insurmountable, but to have the character overcome them anyway. The greater the conflict, the more impressive the effort and eventual outcome. The conflict doesn't have to be on a grand scale – war, for instance – and every decision doesn't have to be life-or-death. Conflict can be internal and much quieter, existing on a quotidian level, small-scale as it is in Anita Brookner's *Hotel du Lac*, but it must be there.

Conflict within a novel can work on many levels. First of all, there is 'personal' conflict, the fight a person has with themselves. This may be the struggle for spiritual enlightenment, as in the case of Herman Hesse's *Siddhartha*, or it

114

might be the result of a dissatisfaction (as it is for Emma Bovary), or a disaffection – Knut Hamsun's *Hunger*, for example. The point is that the main character feels some kind of 'lack', something wanting inside them that drives them to change their state of being. The stories that work on this kind of conflict can be insightful existential 'portraits' of individuals and often produce great character studies.

Secondly, there is 'interpersonal' conflict, the conflict between two people who, for whatever reason, do not see eye to eye. It could be within a marriage, between a pair of aluminium salesmen in 1950s Baltimore (*Tin Men*), or amongst soldiers, as in *Platoon*, in which the two sergeants fight over the soul of a greenhorn GI. This kind of conflict is at its most heightened when it is based on a protagonist and antagonist who have mutually exclusive goals, so that, if the protagonist achieves what they set out to do, it is at the expense of the antagonist, and *vice versa*. One very common example of this kind of conflict is the story of the 'hunter and the hunted', which is the template for count-less *Boys' Own* adventure stories. Alexandre Dumas' *The Count of Monte Cristo*, for instance, or Hugo's *Les Misérables*, in which Javert mercilessly and relentlessly pursues the reformed convict Valjean.

Finally, there is 'social' conflict, which arises between one person and a whole community. In general, this type of story is the result of differently held views, whether it be an individual's non-conformist approach to life (*Crime and Punishment*, for example), or the result a person maintaining their integrity in the face of great hostility, as in *Twelve Angry Men*. The permutations are endless, but all stories with this level of conflict have in common the idea of 'one person against the world'.

There is another level of conflict, namely that between a person and their environment, but as the subject of these stories is usually some form of natural phenomenon, these stories typically don't pay much attention to character. This kind of conflict is to be found in movies such as *Twister*, *Titanic*, *Armageddon*, etc.

One of the reasons the books that make up the Western 'canon' have endured is because they usually work on more than one of these levels; indeed, some of them work on all three. The initial conflict in *Madame Bovary*, for example, is that Emma Bovary is unhappy with her lot. She believes she deserves a better hand than life has dealt her and she begins to take this frustration out on her husband. Although her husband is loyal, tension grows between them. After two desultory affairs, she has debts that she cannot repay. Her name is tarnished and rumours begin to spread about her affairs. She sinks further into debt and is shunned by the villagers. Her original dissatisfaction has spread out and infected the lives of those close to her and contaminated the community she lives in. Rather than face up to her problems, she drinks arsenic and dies a horrific death.

> 'Writing this book I am like a man playing the piano with lead balls attached to his knuckles.' – Flaubert on *Madame Bovary*

When placing obstacles for the characters to overcome, one important point to bear in mind is to ensure that those events don't just happen *to* your characters, but that they happen *because of* them. It is easy, and tempting, just to hurl random impediments at characters, but they should in some way be the result of a character's actions and decisions. If something 'just happens' to a character, and they are not seen to act on or react to it, they will be cast merely as a passive victim of circumstance rather than an active generator of incident. In this instance, you need to ensure that character determines plot, not the other way round. A character must *achieve* their success, not just acquire it.

Plotting your novel is the stage when you should be making sure that your character will not achieve their aims too easily. A good question always to ask yourself when considering this issue is, 'What is it costing the character?' What do they have to give up, exchange, or lose, in order to get what they want? And does it cost them, not only to get what they want, but to keep it, too? Characters must pay some kind of price for what they desire and that cost is our investment in their story. If the price is too high and the character fails, the reader may well feel cheated. If the price is high, but the character succeeds against the odds, the reader will sense the implausibility. If, on the other hand, the cost is too low, the reader will think 'Why bother?' It is vital to make sure it is difficult for the characters to achieve their goals – not impossible, just difficult.

Resolving conflict brings about change within a character and brings emotional satisfaction to the reader. The conflict resolution in a great many of the best-known stories ends in death, but death doesn't always resolve issues and isn't always the natural endpoint of a story. In *The Sheltering Sky*, for example, Port's death in the desert provokes an existential 'panic attack' in his wife, Kit. She is crushed by his death, but she is also liberated. The novel continues for another sixty pages as we see the consequences of Kit's loss play itself out in the narrative and, by the end, we realize that the story has been about Kit all along, not Port. His death has not resolved her life, just set her off on a new and different journey. Indeed, endings of stories are, in a sense, just beginnings to other stories. In the most perfectly plotted stories, resolutions give rise to a new set of problems.

'I don't believe life is about problems and solutions. I believe it is about dilemmas, and dilemmas don't have solutions; they have resolutions, which then morph and lead you into future dilemmas.' – Paul Schrader

If you have plotted your story well, and have placed enough obstacles in the character's way for us to enjoy their eventual success as much as they do, your previously 'flatlining' story will now seem full, rich and well-developed. The ups and downs in the character's physical and emotional journey will resemble the peaks and troughs of an ECG printout and you will have breathed life into your story.

So, have confidence in your characters. Give them adversity to overcome – a love lost, a chance missed, a stranger who comes to town. Let their actions and decisions generate the story and not *vice versa*. Show their inner struggle, their struggle in a relationship, or within a community, and let the reader revel in the hard-earned and long-delayed outcome of your story.

7. Coincidence, Convenience and Credibility

In a story I once read, two young Germans fell in love, but were then separated by war. Twenty years later, the man found himself in New York. He wasn't there on business, and he knew no one in the city – there was no real reason for him to be there at all, in fact. As he was walking down a main street in Manhattan, he thought about his lost love. He knew that she went to live permanently in the USA, but didn't know where. Then, lo and behold, he bumped into her in the street. Amazing! What are the chances? It's a miracle!

Coincidence is one of the first and most insidious traps for a first-time writer to fall into. It all seems so logical and natural that two people should 'just happen' to bump into each other in a city the size of New York but, to the reader, nothing could be further from the truth. It is difficult for inexperienced writers to spot the difference between a character being somewhere for the sake of the plot and a character being somewhere because they have good reason. It was necessary for the young German man to go to the USA so that he could meet his lost love again, so the writer had him go there for no other reason. Returning to Scott Fitzgerald's idea that character and plot are dual aspects of the same function, it follows that a character's arrival at a place must be the consequence of something that happened beforehand and must be the cause of what happens afterwards.

Set down like this, it is clear that there is an inversely proportional link between a character's motivation to go somewhere and a reliance on coincidence to get them there. A surfeit of coincidences in a story is usually the result of a complete lack of character motivation. If, as a writer, you're not sure why characters are doing things, it is tempting to make them 'just happen' to be in the right place at the right time. This is the easiest, laziest route for you to take as a writer. It means that you are not doing your job properly because you are taking a short cut and avoiding the hard work of properly embedding the reasons for your characters' actions.

You may hope that no one will notice, but of course they do. Readers can spot coincidence used to advance a plot at a hundred paces. Just one whiff of such expediency and you will be guilty as charged. Relying on coincidence to further your story will demolish what Coleridge termed the 'suspension of disbelief' and destroy any confidence the reader has in the author's abilities as a storyteller.

It is far more dramatic, and believable, if you give a reason for a character to be in a particular place at a particular time. It would have been far more credible, for example, if the writer had made the man go to great lengths to find out where his lost love was. Perhaps he hires a private investigator, or does the work himself, searching through phone books, city records and employment details, following every clue until, finally, he gets a lead as to her whereabouts. Then, he books a flight and we watch with apprehension as he makes his way over to America to visit her. How will she react? What will she say? Now, the meeting in America is set up, not merely a coincidence. We follow every step of the way as our hero expends a huge amount of energy in search of his lost love. Not only is this whole scene now highly motivated, it is also supremely suspenseful.

Of course, as a writer, you can purposely employ coincidence as a narrative device – a character can still appear to be somewhere coincidentally when, in fact, they are feigning surprise when they 'just happen' to bump into someone, but this shows planning aforethought and so is admissible. Whatever the reason, characters must have *motives* for their actions; they must be seen to be actively determining the course of their own life and not just 'floating' through the story, letting things happen to them. Remember, 'acting is doing', and the story's direction grows out of what the characters *do*.

If you feel that you might have too many coincidences in your story, look back over your manuscript for expressions such as 'suddenly', 'at the same time', 'accidentally', 'luckily', or 'fortunately'. The most culpable of these is 'suddenly', a word that has been the cause of thousands of chance meetings and unexpected events. Go back over your plotting and, at every moment, ask yourself not only *what* happens next, but *why*.

Aristotle makes the distinction between what is possible and what is plausible. A movie does not have to be possible; it has to be plausible. It's not quite possible that the whole story of Oedipus would ever happen; it's only remotely possible. But it is plausible – that is, it satisfies some psychological need in response to a personal notion of what is true. So, therefore, Oedipus is plausible because it *should* be true, or needs to be true, not because it *could* be true. And in the same way any fiction should be plausible, though it need not be possible. – Paul Schrader

The contract between reader and author rests on the reader's willingness to suspend their disbelief. For the sake of the story, readers will accept as believable, provisionally at least, those events or characters that would otherwise seem incredible. So your job is to make sure that your characters and events remain as credible as possible.

Again, this is often where inexperienced writers fall down. The trap lies in not being able to judge how far to stretch the bounds of credibility. For example, in another story I once read, the narrator comments during a knife fight that one of the characters draws a small knife that he had discovered earlier. There had been no prior mention of this knife and so the reader immediately thinks, 'Where on earth did this knife come from?' Later on in the same story, a character gains illegal entry into a building, and the narrator says that he forced the lock and pushed the door open. Again, the reader's first response here is to ask 'How exactly did he manage to do that?' It is actually quite difficult to break into a building, yet the character does so with effortless ease. Characters that move around like superheroes, who are able to go for days without food or water, to travel huge distances on little or no money, produce weapons from nowhere, enter and leave buildings at will – there isn't a level of reality here that the reader can believe in. Moments that stretch the bounds of credibility in this way will be picked up and questioned instantly by the reader. If you don't have the answers, then you have a problem.

These issues of coincidence and credibility are indications that the writer is ordering events to suit their needs, not the needs of the story. As an author, it is convenient for you to have a character achieve everything they need with the minimum of effort and exactly on cue, as it were. 'On cue' is the key here. If you look back over your plot and find that everything is happening more quickly and easily than you had planned, chances are that events are happening far too conveniently to be credible.

The notions of coincidence, convenience and credibility are interchangeable to a certain degree, and are really just part of the same big headache. Again, the trick is to try to shake yourself free of thinking in terms of the easiest, laziest routes. If events happen completely 'on cue', there will be little surprise or suspense for the reader, so throw something in to stir up your plot. Make sure that, however unlikely an event may seem, it stays the right side of plausible by making the event arise as much as possible out of what preceded it as well as precipitating what follows. Finally, make sure your characters have their reasons for the things they do. If done successfully, this work will restore the reader's faith in you. Once you have their trust, you will be able to lead them anywhere you like and, not only will they follow, they will do so gladly.

8. Handling the Passage of Time

'Which is wrong? The weather or our calendars?' – John Cage

In addition to deciding on what kind of role you want your narrator to play in the telling of the story, how you handle the passage of time is the most essential decision you will make as a writer. Because the passage of time is the most 'novel-like' feature of a novel, the thing that defines it *per se*, this is the aspect of fiction over which you need to exert most control.

As we have already seen, all narratives are made up of two time schemes, one inside the other: there is 'the time of the telling' and 'the time of the thing told'; 'narration' and 'story' respectively. This temporal double helix is what defines a narrative – without it, we have either pure description (which is spending time describing space) or pure image (which creates a space within a space). Since there are two time schemes to consider, your decision regarding how to handle the passage of both produces all sorts of permutations.

The French narratologist, Gérard Genette, has looked in detail at these permutations and has written about the main differences between them.

Summary

This is the most common way in which we combine these two time schemes and occurs when the time of the narration is briefer than the time of the story. Most novels simply do not take as long to read as the events in the story took to happen, so the default setting of most novels is that they are 'summaries' of the stories they are telling.

However, there is a more particular use for 'summary' within a narrative, one whereby the narrator decides to offer us a 'round-up' of events *within* a scene in order to speed up the pace of the narrative, a decision which means that the narrator 'glosses over' such scenes instead of 'getting into' them. For example: 'On arrival home Elizabeth went to her room to have a rest, while Teresa unpacked the trunks'; or 'They finished their tea and went to their rooms to get dressed'; or 'After dinner they went to the drawing room. Teresa continued with the letters and her aunt read the newspaper . . .' This device is especially common in nineteenth-century 'classical' narratives.

In these kinds of text, not only does the narrator sometimes sum up events for us *within* a scene, they may also choose to account for all the story-time that passes *between* scenes. For example: 'The next few days passed pleasantly . . .'; or 'During the two weeks after her aunt's death . . .'; or 'Over the following days there was a whirlwind of activity.'

Rather than speeding up the pace of the narrative, the narrator's tendency to 'summarize' the story within scenes, and account for all the time that passes between scenes, actually slows down the pace because, narratively speaking, these moments are 'dead time', *longueurs* when the narrative is merely treading water. Anti-dramatic by nature, they neither drive the story forward nor do they provide enough interest in themselves to justify their inclusion.

One of the golden rules when embarking on a long piece of fiction is that, nine times out of ten, you simply don't need to 'round up' events for us like this, or 'account for all the time that passes'. Instead, cut to the quick of each scene, and cut to the next scene at the first available opportunity, in order to keep the pacing crisp and the story flowing – your readership will be eternally grateful if you do.

Ellipsis

'Encompassing the complexity of existence in the modern world demands a technique of ellipsis . . . I see the art of the ellipsis as crucial. It insists we go directly to the heart of things.' – Milan Kundera

An 'ellipsis' is a period of time left out of the narrative, an elision, an omission. As in the above quotation by Kundera, ellipses in a sentence are usually marked by three dots, or by a line break (not a new paragraph) between sections within a chapter. The important point to bear in mind is that, technically speaking, an ellipsis is a discontinuity in the *narration*, not the story, so when we come to the three dots, or a line break, it does not mean that there is an interval in the story, but it does mean that a period of time has been left out of its telling.

Another point to bear in mind is that ellipses mark a leap in time, but they do not necessarily mark a shift in space. We may 'cut' forward in time, but we may also 'cut' to another place without any time having elapsed at all, so the term 'ellipsis' only refers to a jump in time, not space.

The use of ellipses as a literary device is not new. As Seymour Chatman notes, 'Ellipsis is as old as the *Iliad*.' Henry Fielding famously used it to omit twelve years of Tom Jones' life because 'nothing worthy of a Place in this History occurred within that Period'. As a result of the stodginess that 'summary' can create in a narrative, it has largely fallen from favour, but the ellipsis ensures that narrative flow is kept at a premium and, for this reason, it still retains its sense of freshness and urgency.

A woman arranges to have lunch with her boyfriend and puts the phone down. We then cut to her sitting at the restaurant table – no need to see her get dressed, leave her flat, get on a bus, etc. The idea of *selection* is key. They say you can burn the first two reels (about twenty minutes) of most Hollywood films before the story really gets going, and it is true. Get into scenes as *late* as possible and get out of them as *early* as possible. No need to include the preamble, or the postscript, and definitely no need to report all the details in between.

Scene

Story and its narration are of relatively equal duration here, so the reader experiences the story more or less 'as it happens'. The conventional nineteenth-century novel alternated 'scene' with 'summary' to comprise its narrative, a pattern that many novels have followed ever since. Although many contemporary novels pay much more attention to scenes written in 'real time', it is still rare for a narrative to be written entirely minute by minute. Setting a 250-page novel – which would take approximately ten hours to read – exhaustively around ten consecutive hours in a character's life is a high-risk strategy and, for better or worse, most readers would simply not have the patience to read it.

There are examples of such texts, however – the TV series *24* is an obvious example, but there are other, older examples, too. In 1948, Hitchcock filmed a scene-for-scene version of Patrick Hamilton's stage play *Rope*, which is a real-time account of an evening spent by a schoolteacher, among others, at the house of two of his former students. Hitchcock built an elaborate set that could accommodate complicated camera movement, and filmed in real time, so that the only cuts in the finished film occur when the canisters of film ran out. For a modern audience, the highly theatrical end product is perhaps a little 'creaky', but it is fascinating nonetheless to see every step of James Stewart's gradual realization that the students are, in fact, murderers.

Agnès Varda also used a (there or thereabouts) 'real-time' narrative for her film, *Cléo de 5 à 7* (1961), which shows us two hours in the life of Cléo as she wanders around the streets of Paris, waiting for the result of a medical biopsy for cancer. Naturally, the pleasures of Varda's film do not lie in a strong plot, but she offers various other narrative devices and textures – internal monologue, chance encounters, a strong sense of location, lighting, etc. – to maintain the viewer's interest.

Stretch

The time of the telling in this classification is longer than the time of the thing told. When the narration in a narrative is 'stretched' like this, the effect is similar to looking through a convex lens – the story-time remains the same but the narration expands. Again, it is rare for the narration in novels to be longer overall than the story, but there is an argument for saying that *Ulysses* is such an example. The novel is set over a period of twenty-four hours, but most readers, if not all, are unlikely to be able to finish the book in that time and so the story-time is 'stretched' for its entire duration.

Handling the passage of time in this way is very common for individual scenes, especially those that constitute moments of 'high drama'. At such moments, it is good practice to slow the narration down so that the reader can absorb the full emotional impact of the scene and pick up every nuance of detail – not so much that the scene becomes overwrought, just enough that the reader experiences the full emotional 'weight' of a scene. Key dramatic scenes that pull their punches are very frustrating for the reader.

One of the most famous examples of the 'stretched' scene is the seven-minute Odessa steps sequence in Sergei Einsenstein's film, *Battleship Potemkin* (1925), which is extended to an excruciating degree so that we don't miss a thing. As the soldiers fire and descend on the protesters, we see a woman pick up her skirts and run, a man with no legs leaping down steps, a man taking an eternity to fall, the camera moving with the protesters down the seemingly endless flights of steps, an old man on the ground being jumped over, people rolling down the concrete steps. A young boy, oblivious of his mother, is shot and falls over, but she turns and sees him and screams in terror as someone crushes his hand, and, most famously of all, a pram takes an age to tumble down the steps, forever teetering on the brink of falling over. The whole scene takes longer to happen than would have been the case in reality, creating an unbearable sense of tension.

Pause

This occurs when the story-time stops altogether, although the narration continues. In fiction, this is the case when we step 'out of the action' because the narrator pauses to describe a person, object or place. As we've already seen, the narrative is temporarily no longer a narrative because one of its time schemes has stopped. A different kind of writing now takes over: description, which is time spent describing space. Virginia Woolf's novel, *To the Lighthouse*, has a 16-page middle section entitled 'Time Passes', which is a static description of the Ramsay family's Scottish holiday house over an extended period of many years. There is no action in the section, no dialogue, just a long series of descriptions of the house and its environs.

In cinema, the 'freeze frame' is an example of a moment when the time of the thing told stops completely. The effect of a freeze frame is very powerful, especially if it comes at a film's end, when it is held as the final, climactic note. In François Truffaut's *The 400 Blows* (1959), the final image of the film is a freeze frame that catches 12-year-old Jean-Pierre Leaud as he sees the sea for the first time in his life. After a series of disasters and a life of hardship, his joy on the sandy beach is self-evident as the camera freezes on his face. The effect makes us ponder, even more than usual, what life has in store for this young, but resilient, boy.

In *Butch Cassidy and the Sundance Kid* (1969), however, the final freeze frame is used to create a very different effect. Here, the frozen moment is the moment Butch and Sundance run out, guns blazing, to meet their deaths. By the time the film's inevitable outcome has been reached, the characters of Butch and Sundance have worked their way into our affections so much that the makers decide not to show us their gory end. The final image, capturing the moment they realize the odds are stacked too heavily against them, turns to sepia and is held in perpetuity, thus ensuring mythical status.

The Flashback

We all know what the term 'flashback' means, but, similarly to the concept of 'narrative', try to define it precisely and it soon gets more fiddly than you initially thought. At its most simple, a flashback is a depiction of events understood as having occurred prior to the section that precedes it. It is all to do with comparing time. If a reader were to pick up a book and open it at any point during a flashback, they would not be able to distinguish it from sections of the narrative that were not flashbacks. It is only by temporal difference that we understand what a flashback actually is.

As a literary device, the flashback is nothing new – it, too, is used in the *Iliad*. Genette also did work on flashbacks, and came up with a useful set of terms to differentiate between them. 'Anachrony' is the general term he used for any kind of temporal 'break'. His term for a flashback is 'analepse' and his term for a flashforward is 'prolepse'. 'Interior' analepses refer to any event happening inside the narration but not already shown, whereas 'exterior' analepses refer to events occurring before the narration's beginning. 'Amplitude' is his term to describe how much of the past is told and the 'portée' of the analepse is how long ago the past event occurred.

The flashback is a device that rearranges, and therefore complicates, plot order. Some flashbacks act merely as a 'story being told' and tend not to be very subjective. They add touches to the story, plugging the gaps in our knowledge of what went on in the past. They can, for example, be used retrospectively to fill in ellipses. This is a relatively straightforward usage of the flashback, but other kinds of flashback can be used in a highly interiorized way, producing something far more subjective and embellished. This kind of flashback is typically used as a means of representing memory, dreams or fantasy. Flashbacks can thus be used in a much more elaborate way, as a contributor to the *style* of the novel, not just the story.

When there is a juncture in the narrative between present and past, the join can become a complex interface between memory and history. At that moment, there is the character as a 'subject in history', but there is also the character's relationship with the retelling of his or her past. Whatever we have experienced in life sinks into our memory and is foreshortened by it. Later, it might be called to mind again and set against a different background, with the result that the subject is able to develop hitherto unforeseeable connections between past and present. The memory recalled, however, can never assume its original shape, because this would mean that memory and perception were identical, which is clearly not the case. A new setting brings to light certain aspects of what we had committed to memory and these bits of memory, in turn, shed light on the next new scene or setting we encounter. These connections are the product of the subject's mind working backwards and forwards against each new event. The merging of these two – memory and history – can be called a process of 'subjective memory'.

This is a highly effective means of complicating time and exploring identity. D.M. Thomas' novel *The White Hotel* (1981), is a good case in point, delving as it does into what constitutes 'subjectivity', and how that subjectivity is constructed by historical event and by the individual's reaction to those events.

Thomas' narrative is divided into six parts, the first of which is actually a long, highly erotic, prose poem that we later discover was written on a score for *Don Giovanni*. The second section is a journal, a prose version of the same events. In the third section, Sigmund Freud introduces his case study of a woman called Frau Anna G, an opera singer who has come to him complaining of pains in her breast and womb. Up until now, we have had no reference points to guide us through the story, nothing by which to judge what is 'story', what is 'narration' and what is memory, dream or fantasy.

It isn't until the fourth section, well over halfway through the novel, that we meet the 'real' main character – Lisa Erdman – for the first time. This meeting reshuffles the time schemes in our head and we realize that 'Anna G' is Freud's pseudonym for Erdman and that the first two sections were Lisa's fantasies that Freud had asked her to write down. We deduce that this must have happened after the third section, so we have begun the novel with a 'flashback-fantasy'. This third section, the Freudian case study, explores her deep past and the fourth section returns to the present day. In the fifth section, we once again follow Lisa in the present day as she gets caught up in the general flight from Germany in 1936. The final section is a coda: a kind of dream (a prolepse?), or maybe a wish fulfilment – we are never sure what.

If it shows anything, the oneiric narrative of *The White Hotel* demonstrates that time is once again treated as an element to be shaped and shifted. Temporality is subjective and relative. The novel's exploration of the unconscious ultimately escapes the level of 'psychological realism' inherent in the character of Lisa Erdman and becomes the subject of the narrative itself. The Chinese-box-like structure of the narrative means that we never discover the truth of Lisa Erdman; her character constantly eludes us, just as her own past eluded her.

Flashbacks are alluring devices for first-time writers. They promise lucidity, profundity, but are mostly used clumsily, taking away from narrative clarity instead of adding to it. Flashbacks provide background information, but they also stop the story dead in its tracks. If a flashback is particularly long, or delves too far back in time, it can do irreparable harm to the narrative flow and reading experience.

The key is to use them very sparingly indeed, and only if you feel it is absolutely necessary. If you think you need a ten-page flashback, chances are you don't. If you find that you can only explain an aspect of your story by including a ten-page flashback, you almost certainly need to rework your plot. In my experience, the most powerful way to use flashbacks is to provide just a brush stroke or two to fill in character detail. Plucking a moment out of a character's past that 'cross references' the present-day story, or that provides evidence of a consistency of behaviour over time, can be very effective indeed at increasing our sense of who a character is and why they do things.

As a writer, however, allow time for these decisions to develop in your writing, since they are often best made subconsciously. Flashbacks function on a very different level than plot, say, because not only can they be used to clarify aspects of the story, but they also enhance the fabric of a narrative, adding texture and tone, providing light and shade. If used well, they contribute uniquely to a story.

The Flashforward

'Time interests me tremendously because there is such confusion in it. It is only something we have invented for ourselves. It's a trap. I wanted to destroy that trap.' – Nic Roeg

Pauline Kael described Nic Roeg's 1973 film, *Don't Look Now*, as 'The fanciest, most carefully assembled enigma yet put on screen'. The story centres on a couple, John and Laura (played by Donald Sutherland and Julie Christie), whose daughter, wearing a shiny red mac, has recently drowned in the pond at the family home. They go to Venice, where John is restoring a church, to recuperate. There, Laura meets a blind woman who is a 'seer' and who tells her that her husband is in mortal danger because he refuses to acknowledge that he, too, has the gift of second sight. Meanwhile, not understanding what he is seeing, John has had several sightings of a tiny figure dressed in a shiny red mac . . .

What follows is a series of fragmented clues – glimpses of red, a funeral procession, breaking glass, a cry in the night – all of which meld into an awful sense of impending doom. What John doesn't grasp is that he is seeing the chronicle of his own death foretold. Right up to the very last moments of the story, the funeral procession is puzzling for the viewer – whose is it? We don't understand what we are seeing. Bizarrely, these flashforwards are only understood in retrospect; it is only once we have arrived at the moment in the story from which the flashforward commenced that we understand that it was a flashforward at all, and the film reveals its meaning only at the moment the viewer plunges through the trapdoor into the abyss of madness.

Flashforwards are used far more rarely than flashbacks because they are particularly prone to confusing the reader or viewer, but they can be an effective method of foreshadowing. In Sam Peckinpah's *The Getaway*, a violent criminal called Doc McCoy (played by Steve McQueen) is met by his wife (Ali McGraw) after his release from prison. They go to a motel room, where it is clear there is a great deal of distance between them. In slow motion, we suddenly see them jumping fully clothed into a cool, clear lake. Then we are back in the motel room, the silence between them just as heavy as before. They leave the motel and come across a cool, clear lake . . .

It is only then that we understand that we have seen a flashforward. The amplitude and portée of this prolepse are both very small, but the flashforward serves to give us a 'taster' of what is to come. Jumping into the lake together bursts the bubble of tension between them and they return to the motel room to make love.

9. Pace

When people say a book is too long, they usually mean it is too slow. The pace in a novel is the current in the river, invisible to the eye, but a force on the body. It impacts on readers in subtle, unconscious ways. When readers think they've seen enough of something, but there's more, and no promise of anything changing soon, they can react in a curiously angry way. They can throw tantrums if they are led by the nose at the wrong speed. They need to make their own minds up regarding how fast or slowly they get the hang of your novel – as author, your job is to look at each individual scene and decide on the best pacing to use in order to enhance its action and motifs.

As you would expect, the pace of a narrative has every-thing to do with how you handle the passage of time. Chapters can be short or long, but the pace of a chapter involves more than just its length. How much story-time is covered in each chapter? How long do you take to narrate that amount of story? Clearly, if you take ten pages to account for an hour of story-time, the pace of that chapter will be much faster than if you take twenty-five pages. In addition, there is the 'balance' of the overall narrative to consider. Does the story move quickly in the opening chap-ters, only to tail off in the second half? Does the middle sag?

If you have divided your narrative up into parts, you

also have to think about their overarching combination, their 'architectonic clarity' as Milan Kundera terms it. For his novel *Life Is Elsewhere*, Kundera divided his narrative into seven parts and assigned a musical 'tempo' to each, depending on the relationship between how long the part was and how many chapters it included. Part One, for instance, contained eleven chapters in seventy-one pages, so he labelled it *moderato* – or 'at a slow, moderate pace'. With fourteen chapters in thirty-one pages, Part Two was *allegretto* – 'at a fairly quick tempo' – and so on. The complete list of tempi was: *moderato, allegretto, allegro, prestissimo, moderato, adagio* and *presto*, which translates as medium, quick, quicker, very quick, medium, slow, quick.

Kundera goes on to say that the movement from the *adagio* of the penultimate part to the *presto* of the final part was the key to the novel. For him, that contrast in pace focused all the emotional power of the novel into one final movement. Symphonies have traditionally been composed by alternating fast and slow movements (rather like the aforementioned alternation of 'scene' and 'summary' in classical narratives), usually ending with a fast, happy movement following a slow, sad one. This patterning of pace is common in many novels and highlights the similarity in deep structure between novels and symphonies.

'Speed up for the essential, slow down for the superfluous.'
– Umberto Eco

This slightly perverse quotation by Eco emphasizes the fact that this model of conventional structure is, of course, not compulsory – anyone can play with pace and structure to their heart's content and produce stunning effects. Sophia Coppola's film, *Lost in Translation*, for example, benefited enormously from her highly individual and unusual approach to the editing of the film. Throughout the film, the viewer senses that 'something is about to happen', but it never does. The narrative feels as though it has been made up of the bits of film that other filmmakers would have left on the cutting-room floor. Characters stare out of windows or into space, they wake, surf through endless TV channels, swim pointless lengths in the hotel pool, go to sleep. There is an air of listlessness, boredom and numbness to the narrative that reflects the state of being permanently jetlagged.

In general, writing too much is far more common amongst first-time writers than writing too little, which is no bad thing, since all can be trimmed and 'tucked in' later on. But, as a general principle, be wary of 'overwriting' because it plays havoc with the pacing of your piece. Naturally, cutting can speed up the pace of your piece. If you feel your pacing is too slow, there are a number of things you can do: cut scenes that do not push the story forward significantly; end chapters or sections earlier; trim down scenes made up almost entirely of dialogue; trim individual lines of dialogue; cut lines of dialogue that are repetitious; avoid making the same point many times over in the dialogue; cut any background information, exposition or historical research that isn't absolutely necessary.

The temptation for novice novelists is to spend the longest possible time with each scene, far beyond what they need in order to move the story forward, whereas what you should be doing, without compromising the scene's integrity, is spending the *least* amount of time possible with each scene. As I have said, get into scenes as *late* as possible and get out of them as *early* as possible. Move things along quickly, don't hang about, keep the reader on their toes, make them have to keep up with events instead of forcing them to twiddle their thumbs while you have your characters overstaying their welcome.

10. Signposting

At the beginning of Jon Amiel's 1995 movie, *Copycat*, Sigourney Weaver is giving a lecture about her experiences as a criminal profiler and psychologist working with the police to hunt down and catch serial killers. As she speaks, the camera pans around the audience, picking out faces. Unbeknownst to us, one of the faces is, in fact, the murderer. It is only later on in the film, when the killer's identity is made clear to us, that we think, 'Where have I seen that face before?'

In Peter Høeg's thriller, *Miss Smilla's Feeling for Snow* (1993), Smilla finds a cigar box cunningly hidden in a brick wall by a young boy who has fallen to his death from a roof. There are five things in the box: a knife, a harpoon point, a bear claw, a cassette tape, and a plastic bus pass holder. Smilla knows that these objects were precious to the dead boy, and so are significant in some way in helping to discover how exactly he died, but she cannot see how any of the objects can help her. Later, she plays the tape: it is of a man talking to himself in a language Smilla doesn't understand. There is the sound of cutlery and the hum of a machine in the background, then the tape suddenly cuts to white noise.

Smilla thinks nothing more of the tape – it seems meaningless. Much later on in the story, she decides to get an expert opinion on the contents of the tape. From one hearing, the expert surmises that the man on the tape is in his mid-forties, from Ammassalik, in east Greenland, and uneducated. He goes on to say that the man is describing a journey across ice, and is talking to a European, because he uses English names for locations. The humming in the background is the sound of propellers. The expert can just make out another voice in the deep background. It is a Dane shouting in English. 'Where in the world,' the expert asks, 'can an east Greenlandic hunter sit and talk in a restaurant, where a Dane is yelling in American English, and where you can hear an airport in the background? Only one place. At Thule Air Base.' The expert analysis proves to be correct and provides Smilla with the lead she needs. She flies to Thule Air Base and, from there, solves the mystery of the young boy's death.

The face in the audience, the tape in the box – these are both excellent examples of 'foreshadowing', the narrative device whereby seemingly innocuous objects later on turn out to be of huge significance. It doesn't only have to be an object – it could be a harmless comment, an apparently trivial event, or a person met in passing (as is the case with John Doe in *Se7en*, for instance, whom we unknowingly come across when he appears disguised as a photographer). The 'trick' of good foreshadowing is to get the balance right between 'hiding' this significance at the time sufficiently well so that the reader doesn't guess straight away, and 'revealing' the existence and presence of the object so that, when its importance is finally revealed, we don't feel that it has arrived out of the blue.

Foreshadowing can be a very effective way of creating surprise and suspense in a narrative, so let's look at these terms in more detail.

Surprise

A surprise in a narrative is the result of an expectation that is shown to be incorrect. We thought something was going to happen, but something else does instead – the plotting has 'wrong-footed' us. We think that this new development was unforeseen, but, on reflection, we realize that, had we looked at events from a slightly different angle, it may well have been predicted. Narratively speaking, the operations at work here are subtle and very sophisticated, which is why thrillers (in which the element of surprise is the defining feature) continue to be so hugely popular.

A surprise is the idea of conflict made concrete. Midway through Curtis Hanson's thriller *LA Confidential*, for example, Detective Jack Vincennes visits his captain, Dudley Smith, at his home late one night with a new lead on a shooting at an all-night diner. Vincennes is filling the captain in on this new information when the latter pulls a gun and shoots him dead. This is a huge surprise, not least because playing Vincennes is Kevin Spacey, an actor so well known that we are not expecting him to be killed off so early in the film, if at all.

It transpires, of course, that Vincennes' new information was leading directly to the captain. Hints and clues have been slowly leaked up to this point, but the surprise is so well concealed that nothing could have led us to suspect such a senior figure within the police department. When faced with Vincennes' new lead, the captain has no choice but to act, and this moment of conflict provides the narrative with its biggest surprise. The captain is now revealed as the villain of the piece. In light of this unexpected twist, we assess new clues as the story unfolds, as well as reappraising previous information, until we see that shooting at the all-night diner does indeed lead to the captain. This is good storytelling. In order to work well, a surprise needs to be both unexpected and plausible. Despite its unexpectedness, we realize that it all fits together. If only we had known where to look, we would in fact have seen it coming.

Suspense

Generally speaking, suspense is a delay in fulfilling an established expectation. Whereas surprise acts rather like a small bomb going off in a narrative, suspense is a state of mind, a constant jangling of the nerves, a siren sounding in the narrative. Whereas surprise is all about misdirection, suspense is about delay and it comes in many flavours.

There is the straightforward 'question and answer' type suspense, for instance, in mysteries and whodunits. Mysteries operate backwards, in that the reader and detective are given all the 'effect' of the crime (the body in the library) at the beginning of the narrative and, while moving forwards, must look backwards in time to find out the 'cause' (the murderer). The overwhelming sense for the reader here is a profound feeling of curiosity.

Another kind of suspense operates in 'dramatic irony', however. Here, the conclusion to a story is usually foregone, or at least highly predictable. The hero moves closer and closer towards an ending that is both surprising and inevitable. Because we know more about what will happen to the hero than he does, we are not curious about his situation, but we are very anxious about it. This is the kind of suspense on which Hitchcock built his filmmaking career. We know that the man hiding behind the door with a gun is the 'baddie' – what makes us sweat is that the hero doesn't know the man is there.

The heroes in Hitchcock's films are usually seeking a particular object, the thing that will save the world from impending doom, but Hitchcock attached so little importance to the object being sought that he labelled it the 'MacGuffin'. Whether it be radioactive chemicals (as in

Notorious), a code (as in *The Thirty-Nine Steps*), or microfilm hidden in a figurine (as in *North by Northwest*), its function in the plot remained the same. Hitchcock was more interested in anxious journeys than in endings that satisfy our curiosity.

A further kind of suspense exists in texts in which the character knows more than the reader, usually in the form of a secret buried deep in their past that is eventually revealed. This trait is common to both mysteries and thrillers, but whereas mysteries work by posing a question at the beginning of the narrative – 'Who killed Colonel Mustard?' – thrillers don't start with such a huge narrative question mark. In thrillers, the hero instead stumbles upon the enigma and proceeds from there, living on his wits as he deals with the events thrown at him from all quarters.

The first half of *LA Confidential*, for instance, operates very much as a thriller. In the line of duty, Ed Exley and Bud White stumble across some evidence which points to their captain's involvement in an all-night diner shooting. They proceed with caution, trying to find harder evidence. Vincennes' death is confirmation, and the captain's incriminating secret from deep in his past is finally brought to the surface. From now on, the kind of suspense changes: unbeknownst to Exley and White, the captain had known the reasons for the diner shooting better than anyone, but once that knowledge is unearthed, the narrative switches and becomes a straight 'race against time'.

'Foreshadowing' is a highly useful tool for a writer, especially in genre fiction, but it is another device that takes time to get right. To give hints of things to come entices the reader and sets up an expectation for them, but there is a fine line between enticement and blatancy. Whenever there is a possibility of a surprise or some suspense being generated in a narrative, inexperienced writers tend to scupper their chances by allowing the narrator, or characters, to announce the significance of something 'before the fact'. At moments when clues should be subtly hinted at, they are often turned into 'signposts', with a large arrow pointing to what is going to happen. This, of course, deflates the narrative and robs the reader of any possibility of suspense or surprise.

A story I once read centred on a character who suffered from Poland Syndrome. Very early on, the narrator revealed this fact to the reader, but the character had yet to learn of the fact. When he did find out 100 pages later, he was of course completely surprised, but all the reader felt was irritation at having to wait 100 pages for the character to find this out. This is a rather obvious example, but it is surprisingly common for inexperienced writers to signpost to the reader before the fact that something is going to happen.

11. Trying Too Hard

'Similes are like defective ammunition.' – Ernest Hemingway

They say the most powerful people in the world never have to shout. Their power is so absolute, so unchallenged, that they need never raise their voices. The same can be applied to a narrative – at key dramatic moments, does it have to shout to be heard? Do you have complete faith in your narrator, characters and story? When push comes to shove in the story, are you confident that they will know how to respond under pressure?

When writing a first novel, it is often at crunch moments in the plot that a writer loses confidence and relinquishes control over the narrative. The moment a firm hand is needed to keep the story on course is the very moment inexperienced writers relax their grip and the story wobbles. Rather than trusting the characters and the story to speak for themselves, the inexperienced writer tends to 'wade in' with all kinds of overwrought, over-the-top effects in an effort to ensure that the reader understands the significance of the moment. Instead of *showing* a character's excess, the writer steps in and desperately *insists* that the character is excessive. The resultant prose can be very purple indeed.

All stories have moments of high drama. It might be a

drastic role reversal, an exchange of guilt, a dramatic announcement, a long-dead hero making an unexpected entrance, a death, a birth, a car chase, or a knock on the door – whatever it is, it is usually much more effective to hold back at these moments instead of wading in.

If properly constructed, the drama in a scene should be perfectly able to speak for itself without the writer gilding the lily. A sentence containing phrases such as '... his churning emotions ... sobs wrenched themselves from his heaving chest' is designed to impress upon the reader just how high emotions can get and how deep feelings can run, but there is a huge difference between a character 'emoting' and a character showing emotion. As ever, less really is more.

Take this example: ' "Get your hands off me!" Clarenceux snarled angrily.' You have a triple whammy here – not only is anger implied in the line of dialogue (an imperative complete with a back-up exclamation mark!), but 'to snarl' also implies anger, and then, to top it all off, there is the adverb 'angrily'. The narrator here is trying far too hard to ensure the reader has understood how angry Clarenceux is. Readers are sophisticated people and will deeply resent any form of manipulation or patronizing on the narrator's part – let them make up their own minds as to what they should understand and how they should be feeling.

There are countless ways in which inexperienced writers allow the narrator to make their presence too strongly felt in the narrative.

Tautology

A tautology is a redundant repetition – a 'big hugeness' for example. It isn't only inexperienced writers who use it unwittingly. It is such a delicate distinction that it is almost impossible to notice yourself doing it. Take this observation by the narrator, for example: 'His brown eyes focused intently.' The problem here is that if a person's eyes are focused, this already implies that they are looking 'intently' at something, so the phrase is tautologous. Similarly, the sentence 'That night she tossed and turned, unable to sleep' is tautologous because the expression 'tossing and turning' suggests an inability to sleep.

Adverbs

'Adverbs are a mortal sin.' – Elmore Leonard

There is an idea that adverbs can greatly enhance a verb, but the opposite is usually the case. For instance, when a the narrator says, 'He had a crushingly ruthless look about him', the use of the adverb 'crushingly' does not enhance the adjective 'ruthless'. Indeed, it only serves to diminish its impact. Adverbs tend only to impoverish verbs, not empower them.

Cliché

This is one of the oldest and easiest of all writing traps to fall into. When getting a first draft down, writers can sometimes reach for the first expression that comes into their heads. What you should end up with in the final draft, however, is the sense that the language used is the last thing you have settled on. Again, the habit of using a cliché is often not perceptible to the 'writing self', and only becomes apparent in rereading and redrafting.

The worst offenders are: eyes that are 'large', 'widened' or 'huge' with an emotion; 'furrowed brows'; heads that are 'spinning'; minds that are 'reeling' or 'racing', memories that come 'flooding back'; characters who are 'filled with curiosity', 'deep in thought', 'trembling with emotion' or whose emotions 'well up' or are 'churning'; passion that is 'boundless'; feelings that are 'inexplicable'; chests that are 'heaving'; hearts that 'pound' or that 'beat fast'; breath that is 'bated'. Falling back on such stock phrases, or such hackneyed and saccharine language, is a sure sign that what you are writing is not dramatic, but melodramatic.

'Sentimentality is unearned emotion.' – James Joyce

Stating the Obvious

Occasionally, in an effort to emphasize some act or event, narrators can also tend to state the obvious. By having the narrator fall back on this for emphasis, they are again underestimating the reader's ability to pick these things up for themselves.

Repetition

A narrator's tendency to make sure the reader has under-stood something that is already patently obvious can also manifest itself in the use of repetition.

12. Exposition

The British public loves reading historical novels and it is one of the most commercially successful genres in contemporary fiction. Obviously, if you want to write a novel set in a particular period, you want to try very hard to recreate the time and place in your book convincingly, so you will need to do a lot of research. This is fine, for research can often be one of the most pleasurable and rewarding parts of writing a novel. Spending months in a library locating, gathering, reading and collating notes can turn you into a kind of literary detective. Finding clues, following up leads, stumbling upon hitherto unknown details that, in turn, reveal further clues – this is all deeply satisfying and worthwhile. How you use all this research, all these facts and information, however, is another matter.

Exposition

Notwithstanding all the aspects of fiction we have looked at so far, one of the most important tasks you face as the author of a historical novel is to incorporate your characters fully into the novel's historical context. This is trickier than it sounds, but a narrative that doesn't manage to do so properly rings particularly hollow. In poorly written historical novels, when a character starts talking about events in Poland's history, for instance, or the political situation of the day, they can often lose their natural way of talking and sound as though they have suddenly stepped on to a soapbox, or have stepped straight out of a lecture theatre. In a story I once read, a character spoke about Germany's imminent invasion of Poland using phrases such as 'Yes, these are dangerous times, there is a shadow falling across the land, a darkness ... There is evil abroad ... It's all coming to an end.' Language like this sounds as though it is being read aloud from a piece of propaganda, or as if it is a voiceover in a newsreel, or heard at a political rally; it doesn't sound at all like the kind of thing one character would naturally say to another.

Rather than revealing anything about the person speaking, it feels as though someone else's words have been put into their mouths in order for the reader to understand better how history impacts on the present day, or to understand the full implications of any event. Information outside the parameters of the story that is placed into a narrative in this way, either by the narrator intruding directly into the story or by the narrator placing information into the mouths of the characters, is called 'exposition'. Take this example: 'The plot centres around that chronicle ... We know it could even lead to the queen being dethroned.' As the character himself states, both he and the person addressed do indeed know that the conspiracy could lead to the dethroning of the queen, so why say so? The reason is clear – the author wants to make sure the reader understands what's at stake.

Such expositional ways of disseminating information sound and feel unnatural because the narrator is being allowed to impart information *directly* to the reader, thus bypassing character and story altogether. This device never rings true because it is there purely for the reader's benefit, not the characters', and it draws attention to the fact that the author has been unable to integrate characters success-fully into their historical context.

Instrumental, not Incidental

A good rule of thumb when writing historical fiction is that you must ensure that any historical detail is 'flush' with the narrative fabric. Any historical detail should be channelled and funnelled *through* character, so that things happen *because of* their presence, not *in spite of* it. Characters should be instrumental in the telling of the story, not incidental to it. You are trying to illustrate a historical situation, not just the historical dimension of human existence. We see, for example, what the streets of medieval London look like precisely because a character walks through them and sees those things for themselves. It is very tempting to start scenes with long, verbose descriptions of interiors, furnishings, decoration, clothing, etc., but we will notice these things much more keenly if we see them through a character's eyes. It should be the very presence of the main character that determines histor-ical event, background detail, etc., not *vice versa*.

This issue relates back to an earlier point regarding the passivity of a character. When writing a historical novel, if you don't ensure that all the historical events are chan-nelled and funnelled through character, these two elements can remain divorced from each other throughout the entire novel. In a badly written historical novel, it is symptomatic that very little actually happens to characters directly because of the historical context. That may sound like an odd thing to say about a novel set during the Second World War, for example, in which it would be natural to expect the deaths of many characters due to its wartime setting, but it is often the case that, when you sit down and consider it, no great change is actually brought about within any of the major characters *because of* the wartime setting. It is more the case that, although these characters play out their drama against the most enormous historical backdrop imaginable, it is the times themselves that change more than the characters. Books can be full of the drama of the mid-twentieth century, but it feels as if these events are happening in the background and that the characters remain in the foreground, forever separated from these events and, ultimately, untouched by them.

The issue of researched historical detail, of how much to include, can be seductive and very beguiling. You have expended so much effort in gathering this information and you don't want to let any of it go to waste, so you convince yourself that all of it is necessary. Pride gets in the way. You are determined to show the reader how much research you have done, and so you go about trying to impress them by piling up facts and information. Rather than bringing the reader into the story, however, all you are doing is pushing them away. We want to read a story, not be lectured at.

The best advice I ever heard on the subject was, by all means do as much research as you like, spend months and months on it if you wish, but once you start writing, make sure to forget all about it. Put it clear out of your mind and only refer to it if you're unsure of a detail. The historical setting of your novel should be part of your gut instinct just as much as any other aspect of writing, so let it sink down to that level before you start writing. Your job is not to 'write up' the researched material, but to nail the story itself, because you are writing a piece of imaginative fiction, not a book on history.

Potted History

The same is true when you provide expositional background information on the characters themselves. Traditionally, background detail like this has been communicated to the reader as a 'summary'. Many classic nineteenth-century novels begin with, or have somewhere near the beginning, a potted history of a character's background. Mary Shelley's novel, *Frankenstein*, for example, begins:

> I am by birth Genevese, and my family is one of the most distinguished of that republic. My ancestors had been for many years counsellors and syndics; and my father had filled several public situations with honour and reputation.

This convention was challenged by the Modernists and has been challenged by writers ever since. Ford Madox Ford, for instance, suggested that a 'lumped' summary like this should be dropped in favour of a 'chronological looping'. Vis-à-vis the main character in a book, Ford stated that the writer ought to 'get him in first with a strong impression, and then work backwards and forwards over his past'. Following Ford's suggestion, any background information should be 'sprinkled' along the narrative, as and when it is needed, rather than being 'front-ended' at the beginning. Such distribution of background detail feels more organic because it arises naturally out of the story, instead of being mechanically 'inserted' as a block of summary.

When you look back over what you've written, whether it be researched historical detail, exposition in the form of narratorial comment or dialogue between characters, or background information as lumped summary, the question you have to ask yourself is the same: is this information absolutely necessary to push the story forward? Is the detail about that lovely earthenware cup glazed in gorgeous amber ochre really necessary? What about that page-long description of the gules and azure of the Duke of Norfolk's flag? You love these details in your narrative, so they are the moments about which you have to be the most brutally honest with yourself. Don't stop to admire the scenery – if setting is not conveyed because of a character's presence, or if it is not pushing the story forward, it is expendable, put in merely to please yourself. Kill your darlings. Write the *story*, not the history.

Fictional Biography

Historical fiction has usually worked by taking contemporary characters and then transporting them back in time and superimposing them vaguely into history. Jeanette Winterson's novel, *The Passion*, published as recently as 1988, is an example of this kind of historical writing. Since then, however, there has been a sea change in the ways of writing about history, methods that have produced many different kinds of historical novels.

In the last decade or so, there has been a growing trend for novelists to turn historical record itself into stories. Novels like *Captain Corelli's Mandolin, Birdsong* and *Cold Mountain* all use actual historical events, which are then reimagined fictionally and peopled with invented characters. A branch and development of this idea is one that uses not only real events as their basis, but also real people, although the novelist still puts imagined words into their mouths. A further development still is the novel that uses real events and people, plus extracts of letters or snippets of real conversation that are then put into the characters' mouths. An example is Jay Parini's book of Walter Benjamin's last days, *Benjamin's Crossing*. So widespread and successful has this development been that it is now very hard to go back to writing a historical novel that has imaginary characters performing invented actions in some unspecific past moment.

'History is nothing other than a distillation of rumour.' – Thomas Carlyle

In my own case, Carlyle's quotation was certainly true when I started researching the life of Mata Hari for my first novel, *The Red Dancer*. As I read the various biographies of her, I found that they all contradicted each other, and so I couldn't trust any of them. They all had one thing in common, however, namely that personal reinvention and self-delusion seemed to be the keys to her life. How strongly we identify with historical figures depends on singleness and consistency – the more singular and consistent they are, the more 'knowable' they become – but the life of Mata Hari was neither singular nor consistent. Rather than let that stop me from writing the book, however, I decided to structure *The Red Dancer* around this problem of who exactly Mata Hari was.

I decided that the narrative would be a series of multiple and inconsistent points of view, made up of eye-witness accounts, by people both real and imagined, letters, newspaper cuttings, documents, quotations, interviews both real and imagined, as well as fiction. Living in the public eye as she did, Mata Hari's life wasn't entirely her own to keep. I made her life a 'series of events', some of which she had control over, some of which she didn't.

The narrative is further fragmented by several non-fiction chapters, which serve to arrest and open out the narrative to provide a cultural and social context for the story. They serve to show how the times in which she lived helped shape her life. My ultimate aim was not to take up a position either for or against Mata Hari; rather, I wished to present enough material for the reader to judge for themselves. History itself is made up of contesting stories and the differing stories surrounding the myth of Mata Hari lie at the centre of the narrative.

Life Writing, Memoir and Biography

'History is not what you thought. It is what you can remember.' – W.C. Sellar and R.J. Yeatman

Another form of writing that has proliferated in recent times is 'life writing'. Fictional biography, with its distance between author and subject, can be classified as a type of life writing, but the term also includes memoirs, biographies and autobiographies, all of which imply a closer relationship between author and subject. While seemingly similar, the terms 'memoir' and 'biography' are in fact deceptively different.

Virginia Woolf famously described biography as 'a bastard, impure art' but, despite her ill will, the form has flourished for hundreds of years. With its emphasis on scholarliness, sources and cross-referencing, biography is an attempt to adhere to the cradle-to-grave facts of a person's life, but, as any biographer knows, the 'truth' of a person can prove elusive. Worse still, the truth of a person and the facts of their life often don't match.

Rather than be hindered by this, however, many recent writers have embraced such discrepancies, producing new variations on the theme. 'Memoir' does not claim to be the truth; it is rather an 'impression' of history, one that does not confuse clarity with accuracy. Memoirs have increasingly employed fictional techniques to tell their stories and, in doing so, they render those stories much more immediate than the worst kind of biography, which sticks doggedly to the facts.

Life writing should come with a health warning, however. When it comes to writing about yourself, or about a member of your family, all critical perspective can fly out of the window and the story can collapse. Ethically, it is a very grey area. If, however, you still want to enter the fray, there are a few things to bear in mind.

When it comes to fictionalizing a life, you become many things at once: historian, biographer, archivist, literary detective. If you are writing about a family member, however, your role as a relative must come last if the piece is to make a first impression on anyone outside your family.

While researching, keep detailed notes. When you come to the actual writing, the small details will stand out. It is the small, personal details that will bring your characters to life and make your piece universal.

Try to be as familiar with your material as possible, almost as if you were learning it by heart. Do as much research as you want, but when it comes to the actual writing, try and forget all about it.

When you begin writing, be selective. You have to be judicious in your choice of action, incident, detail, and you have to combine these with skill and care. Try to find a common theme in the wealth of your material – this will eventually become the story. The commonality of theme – the through-line – will carry your reader.

You can, perhaps, include yourself as the narrator, someone to guide the reader through the story. If you take this approach, the way you respond to the unfolding story reveals you as a character and adds an extra layer of interest and complexity to the story. As a narrator, are you reliable? Will you be ironic? Paula Fox's *Borrowed Finery* is a very good example.

While what you're doing is, strictly speaking, neither fiction nor non-fiction, use fictional techniques in the telling of your story. Unlike stories, life doesn't have a strong structure or general themes, so you'll have to impose these onto your material. Devices like building suspense, switching points of view, foreshadowing or unreliable narration can generate enormous power in your story that, perhaps, may otherwise struggle to keep the reader's attention.

Creative Non-fiction or 'Faction'

In recent years, writers have also looked at things other than real historical characters to find good stories. Novelists have turned to scientific discoveries, animals, minerals and plants, or single historic events as subjects for books – *Longitude* by Dava Sobel, *Cod* and *Salt*, both by Mark Kurlansky, *Tulip* by Anna Pavord and Antony Beevor's *Stalingrad*, for example. By applying fictional techniques in the telling of these stories, we have a new 'hybridization' of fiction and authentic social history. In combining these genres, we have a new form, one in which social history is more pleasurable to read and fiction is more knowledgeable.

13. Editing

So you've finished your first draft. Congratulations! It is quite an achievement. You have come a long way. You have already succeeded where many others have failed. Enjoy the moment and have a well-earned rest. Then, when you think you are ready to return to the beginning of your book to start the editing process, don't do anything of the kind. Put your novel away in a drawer and don't look at it again for as long as you possibly can. When she had finished a first draft, Jane Austen used to put it in a drawer, lock the drawer and give the key to a friend with the instruction not to return it to her for one year, no matter how much she asked for it.

So, pat yourself on the back, put your feet up, go out with friends, have a holiday. There will come a time when you feel ready to return to your draft. No one can say when this will be. For William Carlos Williams, it was the moment when 'the conditions under which it was written' had been forgotten. When you do eventually pull it out and have another look at it, the work won't have changed, but you will. The white heat of creativity will have cooled and you now have a clear, cold eye on the work.

> '[The] longer I can stay away before I have to get it to you the better it will be as [it] gives me a whole new chance to see it cold and plug any gaps and amplify where there is any need.' – Ernest Hemingway

The first person you should be writing for is yourself. You should be writing the kinds of book you would like to read but, once the first draft is finished, you have to start considering other people. Writing is for yourself, but rewriting is for others. The purpose of editing is to address the needs of your 'implied reader'. When you edit, you are asking them a series of questions, such as: 'Does this make sense to you?'; 'Do I need more here?'; 'Am I going too fast?'; 'Does it all add up?' The answers your implied reader gives you will be a good marker to work from.

Although it may have been based on some kind of plan, a first draft is still usually written more organically than mechanically. Coleridge talked about a well of consciousness into which everything is dropped, and the act of creation is lowering a bucket and pulling up words and images. Dredging the unconscious in this manner and including anything that surfaces means that first drafts are full of the language you are most familiar with, but which probably doesn't quite convey the thoughts, feelings and ideas you meant. Second and subsequent drafts are when you can ensure that your long piece is as you intended. Editing, revising and shifting material is when the book, hopefully, will assume its natural shape and come alive. As well as keeping your implied reader in mind, this stage is also a way of making your long piece truly your own.

When you're ready to start the editing process, the first thing to do is read your first draft. Don't make any notes as you read, and don't start editing – just read it. Resisting this impulse to start editing is crucial, because it is only when you finish reading the complete first draft that you will know where best to start the editing. A printed version is better than reading it on your laptop. Even better is putting your work into some kind of book format. Whenever I have finished a first draft, I use lulu.com to make a bound, paperback copy for myself. I have found that reading it in

160

the format for which it is intended gives me critical distance and clarity. If you do this however, make only one copy, don't show it to anyone, and destroy it when you've finished with it. Before reading the book, it is also a good idea to take yourself out of the environment in which you wrote it. This will help you arrive at Williams' suggested state of forgetfulness. Go to a café, the park, or a friend's house for the weekend. A change of scenery will re-energize you and give you even more clarity.

'Read over your compositions, and where ever you meet with a passage which you think is particularly fine, strike it out.' – Samuel Johnson

When you have finished reading your draft, read it again, this time making edits, notes, suggestions on the manuscript. At this stage, try not to be too harsh in your judgements. First drafts are always messy, so allow for that. The key to good editing is to do draft after draft, and you won't be able to see in one sitting all that needs to be done.

Look at the plot in general. What happens when you move from one scene to another? Is there forward movement, a momentum? Does the story sustain itself and develop? Do you find events surprising? Are there any holes that need filling? Do you find yourself wondering what happens to a particular character? Perhaps you need to flesh out their story? Are there any loose ends? Do you resolve the characters' dilemmas to a degree that will satisfy the reader but that also leaves room for their own interpretation?

When you're more or less happy with the overall content and placement of scenes, move from the general to the specific and look at them individually. What kind of shape are they in? Do you satisfy the objective of each scene? Does the action in the scene say something about the characters? Is it moving too fast, or too slow? Is it pushing the story forward? Is it doing too much, or too little? If you left it out, would the story be lacking something?

> 'For if the presence or absence of something makes no apparent difference, it is no real part of the whole.' – Aristotle

Cut down your scenes to their bare bones. Ensure that they make their point, but don't outstay their welcome. Then look at the writing line by line. Although each scene needs to serve the story, it should also be as beautifully written as possible in itself. Does each sentence stand up well on its own? When you place two sentences side by side, is there an attraction between them? Do the sentences align themselves to each other? Do they flow well together? Is there a pleasing mix of long and short sentences? Does this create a rhythm? If any sentence seems too long, it almost certainly is – break it in two and see if both parts fit in somewhere. If not, cut one. Work on your sentences until they feel finished, and then polish the words until they shine.

Adjectives are like coins – spend them wisely. Assigning more than two adjectives to a noun causes us to lose sight of the object, not bring it into sharp focus. Cut feeble, fuzzy words such as absolutely, almost, nearly, often, usually, never, seem to, like, just, sort of, pretty, slightly, fairly, quite. Search for stronger, more distinct words. Be precise. Avoid retreating into abstraction, particularly those abstract nouns that describe states of feeling. All we have for a character whose heart has 'turned to stone' is your word for it. We need to see the emotion for ourselves. Be concrete. Show, don't tell.

The most common pattern by far for all writers is to write a lot and then edit the material down. No matter how much they write, however, inexperienced writers tend to be guilty of overwriting. This is the result of trying too hard and indicates a loss of nerve on your part, a failure to trust the reader's imagination. Have faith in your characters and story and resist the urge to pre-empt the reader's enjoyment of these by having the narrator intervene and go overboard in their descriptions, or by adding 'portent', or by being vague about how people feel.

> 'You practically do not use semicolons at all. This is a symptom of mental defectiveness, probably induced by camp life.' – George Bernard Shaw to T.E. Lawrence

Punctuation is the traffic lights of prose, telling us when to move forward, slow down or stop. Use it. Punctuating your work properly is vital to readers because it helps them to move through your work at the speed you intended. It also tells the reader what to link with what, and why, helping them to move in the right direction through your work. The much-maligned and underrated semicolon, for instance, helps you to link ideas without breaking the train of thought; colons, on the other hand, provide 'back-up' endorsements for statements. Colons, semicolons, commas, full stops, parentheses, em- and en-dashes, hyphens and even 'hanging hyphens' all help readers to make sense of your work.

The forbidden use of the so-called 'Oxford comma' – a comma placed immediately before the word 'and' – is outdated. If it adds clarity, especially in lists, use a comma. The apostrophe 's' still causes major confusion when used in conjunction with 'it'. The point to remember is that 'it's' is only ever a contraction of 'it is' or 'it has'. It is never used to mean anything else, certainly not to indicate possession.

Naturally, your spelling and grammar needs to be first-rate. Most computers now have good spelling and grammar checks, though be careful of grammar checks as they can come up with unintentionally hilarious suggestions. In this book, the suggestion for the line, 'Readers can throw tantrums if they are led by the nose at the wrong speed' was 'Readers can throw tantrums if the nose at the wrong speed leads them.'

'When in doubt, cut.' – Ford Madox Ford

If you hit a wall in the editing process, a moment when you simply don't know what's wrong with a scene or how to resolve it, it is often because there is something not quite right with your plotting; it may also be that your characters are not developed enough.

You can create a great deal of confusion in your narrative if you have been too eager to start writing before properly finishing your planning. Nine times out of ten, large structural problems at the editorial stage are the result of weak plotting or weak characterization.

When he thought he had finished writing *The Great Gatsby*, for instance, Scott Fitzgerald was dissatisfied with how short it was – 50,000 words. Rather than being too short, the story was in reality slightly underdeveloped and Fitzgerald's editor encouraged him to fill it out. Fitzgerald went back to work, splicing in an extra 10,000 words here and there. The 60,000-word version is the one we have today and is one of the most 'perfect' novels ever written. So, if you feel the story is underbaked, go back to the planning stage and look again at your story and plot. Do you need to add one or two scenes? Perhaps you need to lengthen some chapters, or cut others completely and write new ones?

'The good parent, like the good author, neither abandons its offspring nor seeks wholly to control or shape them.' – Mary Shelley

As you work, use the conscious part of your brain, but also use the back of your mind. Issues are resolved in the unconscious part of your mind, too. As you shape and shift your material, you will find yourself thinking about it all the time, at the unlikeliest of moments. In a bar, listening to a friend, an idea for a particular scene will pop into your head. Gazing out of the window on a bus, you will stumble across the solution to something that has been evading you for weeks. Have a notebook with you at all times when you're away from your desk and write down straight away every editorial suggestion that comes to mind. Don't leave it till later – write it down now, or else you will surely forget it.

They say a book is not written, but rewritten, and it is true, but editing can seem very daunting at first. Try not to think of the work ahead as an obstruction. The most difficult part of writing is getting the first draft done, so the hardest part is behind you. It is only once a first draft is done that the real fun begins. This is Walter Benjamin's 'textile' phase. Editing can be the most creative part of the whole writing process, the period when your mind is working simultaneously on both micro and macro levels. Start with small, achievable goals. Concentrate on 'local' issues one by one and you will soon find you are also taking on board much larger editorial problems.

Unexpectedly, you might even find yourself coming up with ideas for new projects. François Truffaut said that, when he was writing a screenplay, he couldn't wait to direct it, and that when he was directing it, he was looking forward to editing it, and that when he was in the editing room, all he could think about was writing again. The end of one project can be a launching pad for another. The entire writing process is cyclical.

'When you reach the end of a book you should still find it possible to remember the beginning.' – Milan Kundera

The things that are wrong with a novel are just invitations for you to make it better. If you're good, you know

165

you can be better, but at what point does one know when to stop? The first thing to ask yourself is whether or not you have said what you wanted to say. If you didn't know what you wanted to say in the first place, how will you know you're finished? Just as it's perfectly possible not to edit a book sufficiently, so it's possible to overdo it. All good books are more than the sum of their parts. They have something ineffable about them, a quality which must not become a casualty of the editing process. So, when do you let go?

You will know when you are finished, believe me. The key to making a novel better is to revise continually, moving with due care and attention through successive drafts like the beam of a lighthouse. Print out, read, edit, revise, print out. At first, this work might entail some major structural rejigging, then it'll come down to tightening one or two scenes, but there will come a time when all you are doing is minor 'tweaking', fine-tuning a few words here and there, when you can't find any more obvious passages to cut or places to rework. The book is resisting your efforts, telling you to leave it alone. You realize that what you now have in front of you is very similar to what you originally had in mind. Your desire to make changes wanes. You're very near the end now.

I'm a strong believer that things can always be made better, but perfection can never be attained. Novels are 'perfectible', in the sense that there is perpetual improvement, but 'perfectible' doesn't mean 'made perfect'. A novel is never finished, only ever abandoned. If we arrived at perfection, there would be no further room for improvement, so attaining perfection is a kind of death. The book in front of you is similar to what you had in mind, but not exactly the same. This is as good as it gets.

If you are striving to write the perfect novel, stop now, because you never will, but that doesn't mean that what you have achieved won't impress you. Ideas come and go, you plan and initiate many projects, but the returns are diminishing and sometimes unlooked for. It turns out that what you end up with is richer and stranger than you intended. You leap back in surprise at what is before you. 'This is plenty,' you think, 'this is more than enough.' Time to put down your pen and walk away.

'A novel is a prose narrative of a certain length that has something wrong with it.' – Randall Jarrell

Afterword

'[Narrative] is simply there, like life itself.' – Roland Barthes

Stories help us to understand ourselves. Life hurls random, chaotic events at us from all directions and the only way we can make sense of it all is by assimilating those events into our own personal narrative – the constant dialogue we have with ourselves, asking what something means, how it compares to a similar event, how we feel and what we will do about it, if anything. As events accumulate, we continually construct and reconstruct our life story, we find comparisons and contrasts with previous memories and slightly alter our expectations and ambitions for the future. The act of putting together stories helps to tell us where and how we fit into the world. We are always looking to make sense of the world and will impose a simulacrum of order onto it whenever possible. When we wake each morning, we remake the world and we do this every day.

Writing a novel takes this personal narrative and finds an 'objective correlative' for it, which is, in T.S. Eliot's words, 'a set of objects, a situation, a chain of events which shall be the formula for that *particular* emotion'. You've done that – your novel sits before you. When you think about it, it catches you in its headlights. It surprises you, like glancing in the mirror and, for a moment, not recognizing yourself. It's an unsettling sensation, but also appealing. You're not quite sure which way to look.

You might feel emotionally exhausted after finishing the novel. This is quite common. All that transference of emotion and energy can leave you feeling depleted and low, but your book is alive, which is the main thing. The trust you've placed in your imagination and intuition has produced this magical, improbable, baffling object in front of you. Writing is an extension of the thought process and of living; it is the necessary response to the condition of life. You have made your mark on the world, your *cri de coeur* has been heard. The book is yours, and yours alone, written with your voice, not someone else's, which is perhaps the deepest satisfaction of all.

Now that you've finished your book, the gut instincts that drove you to write it in the first place have left you with butterflies in your stomach – what next? There are all sorts of reasons for a person to write a book. In my literary consultancy work, people often tell me that they are writing for themselves alone, that their book is intended for private use only. If that is the case, why not self-publish? You can set out the book just as you want, choose your own artwork, write your own blurb.

If, however, you do want to show your work to get some kind of feedback, why not join a local writers' workshop? Or attend a week-long writing course, in this country or abroad? By all means show your book to others, but avoid showing it to family members and close friends. You will put them in a difficult, no-win situation. They know you too well to be completely honest, or else you will be especially hurt by any criticism they offer precisely because they are close to you. Whoever you show your work to, remember that any criticism they offer is subjective and not personal. Develop a thick skin, but remain open to the ideas of others. Show it to more than one person. Draw on the positives.

Alternatively, you might consider a creative writing MA.

Courses like these provide you with a high level of organization and contact time, exposure to a wide range of material, as well as a great deal of feedback on your work from peers and tutors. The group workshop central to most creative writing courses is a nurturing environment in which inexperienced writers can get their work into shape. But, be warned, completing an MA in creative writing successfully does not guarantee success in itself. You meet many figures from the industry, and tutors may be able to help, but paying for an MA does not buy a book deal at the end of the course.

If you have already written a novel and approached agents and publishers without success, a creative writing course can be a good way of getting the kind of editorial assistance that you simply don't get any more at most of the large commercial houses. Editorial staff are over-stretched as it is and do not have the time, and creative writing courses have rushed in to fill the gap. The publishing industry has become a very aggressive one, so, if you are planning on sending your novel out, brace yourself. When you are writing a book, you are an artist, but when it comes to trying to publish it, you have to become a businessman or woman.

Whatever your next step is, there will hopefully come a time when you find that something else pops into your mind and keeps bothering you, like a stone in your shoe. It could be that bizarre story you heard at a dinner six months ago, or an image from a novel that has left a deep impression. This is the next book coming round the corner and knocking on your door. If you are ready, able and willing to experience the frustration, elation, hard graft, inspiration, perplexity and satisfaction all over again, then you could be about to begin the whole process once more.

Writing is a discipline with no end in sight and writers never retire. We write books in order to make sense of our lives and to show the reader some aspect of their own lives that had hitherto remained undisclosed. Books are mirrors, whether we write them or read them. In the end, it is all part of the same process. Having written your book will fill you with joy and wonder, but you will also feel anxiety as it makes its way in the world. How will it fare? What can you do to help? You have very little control over this stage. You have loosed your arrow and now have to wait and see where it falls. Support your book when it is down, revel in its success when it is up, but success and failure are, indeed, both imposters. The work is all, it is we who walk away.

'The artist must make posterity believe he never lived.' – Flaubert

Bibliography

Aristotle; 'Ars Poetica' in *Aristotle/Horace/Longinus: Classical Literary Criticism*, trans. by T.S. Dorsch (Penguin, 1965)

Auster, Paul; *The Art of Hunger* (Faber, 1998)

Barthes, Roland; 'The Death of the Author' in *Image-Music-Text* (Macmillan, 1977)

Bazin, André; *What is Cinema?* Vols. 1 and 2, trans. by H. Gray (University of California Press, 1967 and 1971)

Bell, Julia, and Magrs, Paul (eds.); *The Creative Writing Coursebook* (Macmillan, 2001)

Bresson, Robert; *Notes on the Cinematographer* (Quartet Encounters, 1986)

Chatman, Seymour; *Antonioni, or the Surface of the World* (University of California Press, 1985)

Chatman, Seymour; *Story and Discourse: Narrative Structure in Fiction and Film* (Cornell University Press, 1978)

Field, Syd; *Screenplay: The Foundations of Screenwriting* (Bantam Doubleday Dell, 1998)

Hemingway, Ernest; *On Writing*, ed. by Larry W. Phillips (Granada, 1985)

Iser, Wolfgang; 'The reading process: a phenomenological approach' in *Modern Criticism and Theory*, ed. by David Lodge (Longman, 1988)

Jakobson, Roman; 'The metaphoric and metonymic poles' in *Modern Criticism and Theory*, ed. by David Lodge (Longman, 1988)

James, Henry; 'The Art of Fiction' in *The Portable Henry James*, ed. by John Auchard (Penguin, 2004)

Kundera, Milan; *The Art of the Novel* (Faber, 1988)

Mamet, David; *On Directing Film* (Faber, 1991)

McQuillan, Martin (ed.); *The Narrative Reader* (Routledge, 2000)

Pollack, Sydney; 'Acting is Doing' in *Protections 3* (Faber, 1994)

Pound, Ezra; 'A Retrospect' in *Poetry in Theory: An Anthology 1900–2000*, ed. by Jon Cook (Blackwell Publishing, 2004)

Propp, Vladimir; 'Morphology of the Folktale' (University of Texas Press, 1928)

Robbe-Grillet, Alain; 'Riddles and Transparencies in Raymond Roussel' in *Raymond Roussel: Life, Death and Works* (Atlas Press, 1987)

Sayers, Dorothy L.; 'Aristotle on Detective Fiction' in *Unpopular Opinions* (Victor Gollancz, 1946)

Schrader, Paul; *Transcendental Style in Film: Ozu, Bresson, Dreyer* (Da Capo Press, 1972)

Shklovsky, Victor; 'Art as Technique' in *Modern Criticism and Theory*, ed. by David Lodge (Longman, 1988)

Sontag, Susan; 'Against Interpretation', 'On Style' and 'Spiritual style in the films of Robert Bresson' in *Against Interpretation* (Vintage, 2001)

Index of Names